FIRST GREEK GRAMMAR.

BY

W. GUNION RUTHERFORD, B.A.,

LATE WARNER EXHIBITIONER, BALLIOL COLLEGE, OXFORD;

ASSISTANT MASTER OF ST. PAUL'S SCHOOL, LONDON.

NEW EDITION, ENLARGED.

London:

MACMILLAN AND CO.

1880.

PREFACE.

This First Greek Grammar differs from others in some important respects. It is compiled on a new principle and contains much matter which has hitherto not appeared in elementary books, and some facts that are the fruits of independent research.

The First Part comprises only such forms as it is necessary for a beginner to know, and these are put as clearly and succinctly as the nature of the case allows. Every effort was made to avoid the necessity of explanations in English,—to make in fact the lesson for the day appear as short as possible to the jealous eye of the pupil, while at the same time the local memory or memory of the eye, which is so strong in youth, might be brought as largely as possible into play.

In the teaching of a synthetic language like Greek or Latin, practical schoolmasters are not likely to underestimate the importance of drill in grammatical forms. In such languages the relation between the different words of a sentence can never be clearly understood till the learner becomes thoroughly familiar with the principal inflexions. Familiarity with the accidence is the first step towards appreciative translation. It is true that some boys can learn inflexions with ease who are never able to acquire facility in translation, but it is equally true that without a preçise knowledge of grammatical forms even an intelligent boy loses much of the crispness of the thought.

My original design was thus merely to provide a drill book for beginners, more accurately compiled than those generally in use. Further information each master might impart for himself. But the success of the book prompted me to add a Second Part which should supply remarks on the forms included in the First Part, as well as additional matter of a more advanced kind. In this way much has been added which is not to be found in ordinary Grammars, and the relegation of the paradigms to a separate part has enabled me to discuss interesting points of Grammar in a way which would otherwise have been impossible. Such Chapters as the Third, the Twelfth, and the Seventeenth will, it is hoped, be especially useful in awakening an intelligent interest in a subject too apt to become dull.

Different teachers will have different methods of teaching the Second Part. My own system is gradually to impart additional information contemporaneously with the drill in inflexions. If this is done the pupil finds that little is left for him to learn when he comes to the Second Part.

I have thought it prudent to leave unaltered many forms which usually, though wrongly, find a place in Greek paradigms, as few Greek texts have yet been brought into harmony with the latest results of critical scholarship. I have even retained for the sake of old association such absurd forms as the Imperative λέλυκε. The time will come when they will disappear from Greek Grammars, but an Elementary Grammar is not the place in which first to omit them.

I regret that an accelerated sale made it necessary to reprint the First Part before any corrections were made, but all errors will be carefully eliminated as soon as another opportunity occurs.

W. GUNION RUTHERFORD.

January 1880.

CONTENTS.

PART I.

PART II.

FIRST GREEK GRAMMAR.

LETTERS.

I. THE Greek letters were twenty-four in number.

Α	α	Alpha	=	a.
Β	β	Beta	=	b.
Γ	γ	Gamma	=	g. Always hard.
Δ	δ	Delta	=	d.
Ε	ε	Epsīlon	=	e.
Ζ	ζ	Zeta	=	z.
Η	η	Eta	=	ē.
Θ	θ	Theta	=	th.
Ι	ι	Iota	=	i.
Κ	κ	Kappa	=	k.
Λ	λ	Lambda	=	l.
Μ	μ	Mu	=	m.
Ν	ν	Nu	=	n.
Ξ	ξ	Xi	=	x (= ks).
Ο	ο	Omicron	=	ŏ.
Π	π	Pi	=	p.
Ρ	ρ	Rho	=	rh, r.
Σ	σ ς	Sigma	=	s. ς only at the end of a word.
Τ	τ	Tau	=	t.
Υ	υ	Upsīlon	=	ü.
Φ	φ	Phi	=	ph.
Χ	χ	Chi	=	kh.
Ψ	ψ	Psi	=	ps.
Ω	ω	Omĕga	=	ō.

B

II. Before κ, γ, χ, and ξ the letter γ has the sound of ν.

III.—VOWELS. The vowels are divided into hard, α, ϵ η, o ω, and into soft, ι, υ.

IV.—CONSONANTS. The most important are those consonants which are called Mutes, because we are not able to pronounce them without the help of a vowel. They are nine in number. Three are pronounced by the throat, three by the lips, and three by bringing the tongue against the teeth.

	Hard.	Soft.	Aspirated.
Gutturals or Throat-sounds.	κ	γ	χ
Labials or Lip-sounds . . .	π	β	ϕ
Dentals or Tooth-sounds.	τ	δ	θ

From this table we see that they are again divided into sets of three, each set containing a guttural, a dental, and a labial.

The letters ξ, ψ, and ζ are called double letters: for $\xi = \kappa\sigma$, $\psi = \pi\sigma$, and $\zeta = \delta$ with a soft σ.

V.—SIGNS. The Greeks had no letter like the Latin or English *h*, but they had a sign ʽ which served instead.

Thus ὥρα was pronounced *hōra*, and the sign is always so written over the vowel to which it belongs. This sign is called *spiritus asper*, or rough breathing. ρ is the only consonant with which it is used, and when ρ begins a word it is never without it. If the vowel υ begins a word it has always this sign.

The sign ʼ simply marks the absence of the *spiritus asper.*

DECLENSION OF SUBSTANTIVES AND ADJECTIVES.

VI.—The inflexion of nouns and pronouns is called declension. The fixed part of the word is called the stem, the changeable part is called the case-ending or termination. The nominative case must never be confounded with the stem.

VII.—The Greeks distinguished in declension :

(1) Three Numbers :—The Singular for one, the Dual for two, or a pair, and the Plural for several.

(2) Five Cases :—Nominative, Vocative, Accusative, Genitive, Dative.

(3) Three Genders :—Masculine, Feminine, Neuter.

VIII.—All these, except the vocative case, are seen in the declension of the article 'the.'

		Masculine.	Feminine.	Neuter.
Singular.	Nom.	ὁ	ἡ	τό
	Acc.	τόν	τήν	τό
	Gen.	τοῦ	τῆς	τοῦ
	Dat.	τῷ	τῇ	τῷ
Dual.	N. A.	τώ	τά	τώ
	G. D.	τοῖν	ταῖν	τοῖν
Plural.	Nom.	οἱ	αἱ	τά
	Acc.	τούς	τάς	τά
	Gen.	τῶν	τῶν	τῶν
	Dat.	τοῖς	ταῖς	τοῖς

IX.—Declensions are arranged according to the last letter of the stem. The First Declension includes all stems ending in α (or η): the Second Declension stems in ο (or ω); the third declension stems ending in other letters.

FIRST DECLENSION.

X.—The First Declension contains only masculine and feminine stems. Examples: χωρα, f. *country*; τιμα, f. *honour*; γλωσσα, f. *tongue*; ταμια, m. *steward*; Ἑρμη, m. *Hermes*; κριτα, m. *judge*.

		FEMININES.			MASCULINES.		
Singular.	Nom.	χώρᾱ	τιμή	γλῶσσᾰ	ταμία-ς	Ἑρμῆς	κριτής
	Voc.	χώρᾱ	τιμή	γλῶσσᾰ	ταμίᾱ	Ἑρμῆ	κριτᾰ́
	Acc.	χώρᾱν	τιμήν	γλῶσσᾰν	ταμίᾱν	Ἑρμῆν	κριτήν
	Gen.	χώρᾱς	τιμῆς	γλώσσης	ταμίου	Ἑρμοῦ	κριτοῦ
	Dat.	χώρᾳ	τιμῇ	γλώσσῃ	ταμίᾳ	Ἑρμῇ	κριτῇ
Dual.	N.A.V.	χώρᾱ	τιμᾱ́	γλώσσᾱ	ταμίᾱ	Ἑρμᾶ	κριτᾱ́
	G. D.	χώραιν	τιμαῖν	γλώσσαιν	ταμίαιν	Ἑρμαῖν	κριταῖν
Plural.	N. V.	χῶραι	τιμαί	γλῶσσαι	ταμίαι	Ἑρμαῖ	κριταί
	Acc.	χώρᾱς	τιμάς	γλώσσᾱς	ταμίᾱς	Ἑρμᾶς	κριτάς
	Gen.	χωρῶν	τιμῶν	γλωσσῶν	ταμιῶν	Ἑρμῶν	κριτῶν
	Dat.	χώραις	τιμαῖς	γλώσσαις	ταμίαις	Ἑρμαῖς	κριταῖς

Obs.—1. η of the Nom. Sing. is kept in all cases of the Sing.

Obs.—2. α after a vowel or ρ is kept in all cases.

Obs.—3. α after any consonant but ρ is changed into η in the Gen. and Dat. Sing.

Obs.—4. Nouns in -της, compound words, and names of peoples have ᾰ in the Voc. Sing.

SECOND DECLENSION.

XI.—Stems. λογο, m. *speech*; συκο, n. *fig*; πλοο, m. *voyage*; ὀστεο, n. *bone*.

		UNCONTRACTED.		CONTRACTED.			
Singular.	Nom.	λόγος	σῦκον	πλόος	πλοῦς	ὀστέον	ὀστοῦν
	Voc.	λόγε	σῦκον	πλόε	πλοῦ	ὀστέον	ὀστοῦν
	Acc.	λόγον	σῦκον	πλόον	πλοῦν	ὀστέον	ὀστοῦν
	Gen.	λόγου	σύκου	πλόου	πλοῦ	ὀστέου	ὀστοῦ
	Dat.	λόγῳ	σύκῳ	πλόῳ	πλῷ	ὀστέῳ	ὀστῷ
Dual.	N.V.A.	λόγω	σύκω	πλόω	πλώ	ὀστέω	ὀστώ
	G. D.	λόγοιν	σύκοιν	πλόοιν	πλοῖν	ὀστέοιν	ὀστοῖν
Plural.	N. V.	λόγοι	σῦκᾰ	πλόοι	πλοῖ	ὀστέᾰ	ὀστᾶ
	Acc.	λόγους	σῦκᾰ	πλόους	πλοῦς	ὀστέᾰ	ὀστᾶ
	Gen.	λόγων	σύκων	πλόων	πλῶν	ὀστέων	ὀστῶν
	Dat.	λόγοις	σύκοις	πλόοις	πλοῖς	ὀστέοις	ὀστοῖς

XII.—Words in *-ον* are always neuter. Words in *-ος* are generally masculine; but names of trees, lands, cities, and islands are feminine. Also the following words:—

ψῆφος *pebble*	ψάμμος *sand*	πλίνθος *brick*	σποδός *ashes*
κέλευθος *walk*	ἀτρᾰπός *path*	*and*	ὁδός *way*
ληνός *vat*	σορός *coffin*	γνάθος *jaw*	νόσος *disease*
βίβλος *book*	ῥάβδος *staff*	τάφρος *ditch*	δρόσος *dew*
δοκός *beam*	ἤπειρος *continent*	βάσᾰνος *touch-stone*	
νῆσος *island*	κάμῑνος *oven*	γέρᾰνος. *crane.*	

XIII.—The following nouns are heterogeneous:—

δεσμός, *fetter.*	Pl. δεσμοί or δεσμά.
λύχνος *lamp.*	Pl. λύχνοι or λύχνα.
σταθμός, *stable.*	Pl. σταθμοί or σταθμά.
σῖτος, *food.*	Pl. σῖτα.

XIV.—The Vocative of θεός, God, is always the same as the Nom. In other words, the Nom. is sometimes used for the Voc.

XV.—A few stems instead of *ο* have *ω*. This *ω* takes the case-endings as far as possible.

STEMS.—*νεω*, m. *temple*; *ἀνωγεω*, n. *upper-room*.

Singular.	N. V.	νεώς	ἀνώγεων
	Acc.	νεών	ἀνώγεων
	Gen.	νεώ	ἀνώγεω
	Dat.	νεῴ	ἀνώγεῳ
Dual.	N. A. V.	νεώ	ἀνώγεω
	G. D.	νεῴν	ἀνώγεῳν
Plural.	N. V.	νεῴ	ἀνώγεω
	Acc.	νεώς	ἀνώγεω
	Gen.	νεών	ἀνώγεων
	Dat.	νεῴς	ἀνώγεῳς

THIRD DECLENSION.

I. CONSONANT STEMS.

A. STEMS IN GUTTURALS κ, γ, χ.

XVI.—Stems. φυλᾰκ, m. *guard*; μαστῑγ, f. *whip*; ὀνῠχ, m. *nail*.

Singular.	Nom. } Voc. }	φύλαξ for φύλακ-ς	μάστιξ for μάστιγ-ς	ὄνυξ for ὄνυχ-ς
	Acc.	φύλακ-ᾰ	μάστιγ-ᾰ	ὄνυχ-ᾰ
	Gen.	φύλακ-ος	μάστιγ-ος	ὄνυχ-ος
	Dat.	φύλακ-ῐ	μάστιγῐ	ὄνυχ-ῐ
Dual.	N.A.V.	φύλακ-ε	μάστιγ-ε	ὄνυχ-ε
	G. D.	φυλάκ-οιν	μαστίγ-οιν	ὀνύχ-οιν
Plural.	N.V.	φύλακ-ες	μάστιγ-ες	ὄνυχ-ες
	Acc.	φύλακ-ᾰς	μάστιγ-ᾰς	ὄνυχ-ᾰς
	Gen.	φυλάκ-ων	μαστίγ-ων	ὀνύχ-ων
	Dat.	φύλαξι(ν) for φύλακ-σι(ν)	μάστιξι(ν) for μάστιγ-σι(ν)	ὄνυξι(ν) for ὄνυχ-σι(ν)

B.—STEMS IN LABIALS, π, β.

XVII.—STEMS, γῡπ, m. *vulture;* φλεβ, f. *vein.*

Singular.	Nom. / Voc.	γύψ for γύπ-ς	φλέψ for φλέβ-ς
	Acc.	γῦπ-ᾰ	φλέβ-ᾰ
	Gen.	γυπ-ός	φλεβ-ός
	Dat.	γυπ-ῐ́	φλεβ-ῐ́
Dual.	N. A. V.	γῦπ-ε	φλέβ-ε
	G. D.	γυπ-οῖν	φλεβ-οῖν
Plural.	N. V.	γῦπ-ες	φλέβ-ες
	Acc.	γῦπ-ᾰς	φλέβ-ᾰς
	Gen.	γυπ-ῶν	φλεβ-ῶν
	Dat.	γυψί(ν) for γυπ-σί(ν)	φλεψί(ν) for φλεβ-σί(ν)

All these stems are masculine or feminine.

C.—STEMS IN DENTALS τ, δ, θ.

1. MASCULINE AND FEMININE.

XVIII.—STEM, ἐρωτ, m. *love;* λαμπᾰδ, f. *torch;* κορῠθ, f. *helmet.*

Singular.	N. V.	ἔρω-ς	λαμπά-ς	κόρυ-ς
	Acc.	ἔρωτ-ᾰ	λαμπάδ-ᾰ	κόρυθ-ᾰ
	Gen.	ἔρωτ-ος	λαμπάδ-ος	κόρῠθ-ος
	Dat.	ἔρωτ-ῐ	λαμπάδ-ῐ	κόρῠθ-ῐ
Dual.	N.V.A.	ἔρωτ-ε	λαμπάδ-ε	κόρῠθ-ε
	G. D.	ἐρώτ-οιν	λαμπάδ-οιν	κορύθ-οιν
Plural.	N. V.	ἔρωτ-ες	λαμπάδ-ες	κόρῠθ-ες
	Acc.	ἔρωτ-ᾰς	λαμπάδ-ᾰς	κόρῠθ-ᾰς
	Gen.	ἐρώτ-ων	λαμπάδ-ων	κορύθ-ων
	Dat.	ἔρω-σι(ν)	λαμπά-σι(ν)	κόρῠ-σι(ν)

Obs.—The dentals are dropped before ς. Hence λαμπάς for λαμπαδς, and λαμπάσι for λαμπαδσι.

2. NEUTERS.

STEM, *σωματ*, *body*.

Singular.	N. V. A.	σῶμα
	Gen.	σώματ-ος
	Dat.	σώματ-ῐ
Dual.	N. V. A.	σώματ-ε
	G. D.	σωμάτ-οιν
Plural.	N. V. A.	σώματ-ᾰ
	Gen.	σωμάτ-ων
	Dat.	σώμα-σι(ν)

DENTAL STEMS IN *ντ*.

XIX.—Stems, Αἰαντ, m. *Ajax*; γεροντ, m. *old-man*; ὀδοντ, m. *tooth*.

Singular.	Nom.	Αἴᾱ-ς	γέρων	ὀδού-ς
	Voc.	Αἴᾱ-ς	γέρον	ὀδού-ς
	Acc.	Αἴαντ-ᾰ	γέροντ-ᾰ	ὀδόντ-ᾰ
	Gen.	Αἴαντ-ος	γέροντ-ος	ὀδόντ-ος
	Dat.	Αἴαντ-ῐ	γέροντ-ῐ	ὀδόντ-ῐ
Dual.	N.V.A.	Αἴαντ-ε	γέροντ-ε	ὀδόντ-ε
	G. D.	Αἰάντ-οιν	γερόντ-οιν	ὀδόντ-οιν
Plural.	N. V.	Αἴαντ-ες	γέροντ-ες	ὀδόντ-ες
	Acc.	Αἴαντ-ᾰς	γέροντ-ᾰς	ὀδόντ-ᾰς
	Gen.	Αἰάντ-ων	γερόντ-ων	ὀδόντ-ων
	Dat.	Αἴᾱ-σι(ν)	γέρου-σι(ν)	ὀδοῦ-σι(ν)

All these stems are masculine.

Obs. 1.—When *ντ* is dropped before sigma, *α*, *ι*, *υ* are simply lengthened; *ε* and *ο* become *ει* and *ου*.

Obs. 2.—The vocative has sometimes the pure stem as nearly as possible; sometimes it is like the nominative.

STEMS IN DENTAL ν.

XX.—STEMS, Ἑλλην, m. *Greek*; ποιμεν, m. *shepherd*; ἀγων, m. *contest*; ἡγεμον. m. *leader*; δελφῑν, m. *dolphin*.

Singular.	N. V.	Ἕλλην	ποιμήν	ἀγών	ἡγεμών	δελφις
	Acc.	Ἕλλην-ᾰ	ποιμέν-ᾰ	ἀγῶν-ᾰ	ἡγεμόν-ᾰ	δελφῖν-ᾰ
	Gen.	Ἕλλην-ος	ποιμέν-ος	ἀγῶν-ος	ἡγεμόν-ος	δελφῖν-ος
	Dat.	Ἕλλην-ῐ	ποιμέν-ῐ	ἀγῶν-ῐ	ἡγεμόν-ῐ	δελφῖν-ῐ
Dual.	N.V.A.	Ἕλλην-ε	ποιμέν-ε	ἀγῶν-ε	ἡγεμόν-ε	δελφῖν-ε
	G. D.	Ἑλλήν-οιν	ποιμέν-οιν	ἀγών-οιν	ἡγεμόν-οιν	δελφίν-οιν
Plural.	N. V.	Ἕλλην-ες	ποιμέν-ες	ἀγῶν-ες	ἡγεμόν-ες	δελφῖν-ες
	Acc.	Ἕλλην-ᾰς	ποιμέν-ᾰς	ἀγῶν-ᾰς	ἡγεμόν-ας	δελφῖν-ᾰς
	Gen.	Ἑλλήν-ων	ποιμέν-ων	ἀγών-ων	ἡγεμόν-ων	δελφίν-ων
	Dat.	Ἕλλη-σι(ν)	ποιμέ-σι(ν)	ἀγῶ-σι(ν)	ἡγεμό-σι(ν)	δελφῖ-σι(ν)

Most of these Stems are masculine.

The Vocative is generally the same as the Nom. Sometimes it is the pure stem, as χελιδόν (Nom. χελιδών, *f.* swallow). In two words the last vowel of the stem is shortened. Ἄπολλον (stem, Ἀπολλων), O Apollo; and Πόσειδον (stem Ποσειδων), O Poseidōn.

STEMS IN LIQUIDS λ AND ρ.

XXI.—Stems, ἁλ, m. *salt;* ῥητορ, m. *orator;* θηρ, m. *wild-beast;* μητερ, f. *mother.*

Singular.	Nom.	ἅλ-ς	ῥήτωρ	θήρ	μήτηρ
	Voc.	ἅλ-ς	ῥήτορ	θήρ	μῆτερ
	Acc.	ἅλ-ᾰ	ῥήτορ-ᾰ	θῆρ-ᾰ	μητέρ-ᾰ
	Gen.	ἁλ-ός	ῥήτορ-ος	θηρ-ός	μητρ-ός
	Dat.	ἁλ-ί	ῥήτορ-ῐ	θηρ-ί	μητρ-ί
Dual.	N.V.A.	ἅλ-ε	ῥήτορ-ε	θῆρ-ε	μητέρ-ε
	G. D.	ἁλ-οῖν	ῥητόρ-οιν	θηρ-οῖν	μητέρ-οιν
Plural.	N. V.	ἅλ-ες	ῥήτορ-ες	θῆρ-ες	μητέρ-ες
	Acc.	ἅλ-ᾰς	ῥήτορ-ᾰς	θῆρ-ᾰς	μητέρ-ᾰς
	Gen.	ἁλ-ῶν	ῥητόρ-ων	θηρ-ῶν	μητέρ-ων
	Dat.	ἁλσί(ν)	ῥήτορ-σι(ν)	θηρ-σί(ν)	μητρά-σι(ν)

Of these the stems in -τηρ and -τορ are generally masculine. ἁλ is the only stem in λ.

All stems in ρ form the Nom. Sing. without sigma, but ε before ρ is lengthened to η, and ο to ω.

The Voc. Sing. has the pure stem, but the stem σωτηρ, *saviour,* shortens η to ε, Voc. σῶτερ.

Like μήτηρ are declined πάτηρ (st. πατερ), *father;* θυγάτηρ (st. θυγατερ), *daughter;* γάστηρ, f. (st. γαστερ), belly ; Δημήτηρ (st. Δημητερ), *Demeter.*

II. VOWEL STEMS.

XXII.—Stems in soft vowels ι and υ.

MASCULINES AND FEMININES.

STEMS. πολῐ, f. *city*; σῠ, m. or f. *pig*; πηχῠ, m. *forearm*.

Singular.	Nom.	πόλι-ς	σῦ-ς	πῆχυ-ς
	Voc.	πόλι	σῦ	πῆχυ
	Acc.	πόλι-ν	σῦ-ν	πῆχυ-ν
	Gen.	πόλεως (ε-ος)	σῠ-ός	πήχεως (ε-ος)
	Dat.	πόλει (ε-ϊ)	σῠ-ΐ	πήχει (ε-ϊ)
Dual.	N.V.A.	πόλε-ε	σῡ́-ε	πήχε-ε
	G. D.	πολέ-οιν	σῠ-οῖν	πηχέ-οιν
Plural.	N. V.	πόλεις (ε-ες)	σῡ́-ες	πήχεις (ε-ες)
	Acc.	πόλεις (ε-ας)	σῦς (σῡ́-ας)	πήχεις (ε-ας)
	Gen.	πόλε-ων	σῠ-ῶν	πήχε-ων
	Dat.	πόλε-σι(ν)	σῠ-σί(ν)	πήχε-σι(ν)

The Nom. of some of these nouns is generally used instead of the Voc. Thus we almost always find ὦ πόλις.

NEUTERS.

STEM. ἀστυ, *city.*

Singular.	N. V. A.	ἄστυ
	Gen.	ἄστεως (ε-ος)
	Dat.	ἄστει (ε-ϊ)
Dual.	N. V. A.	ἄστε-ε
	G. D.	ἀστέ-οιν
Plural.	N. V. A.	ἄστη (ε-α)
	Gen.	ἀστέ-ων
	Dat.	ἄστε-σι(ν)

Most stems in *ι*, and some in *υ*, change the vowel to ε in the Gen. and Dat. Sing., and in all cases of Dual and Pl.

XXIII.—Stems in ευ, αυ, ου.

STEMS. βασιλευ, m. *king;* γραυ, f. *old-woman;* βου, m. and f. *ox.*

Singular.	Nom.	βασιλεύ-ς	γραῦ-ς	βοῦ-ς
	Voc.	βασιλεῦ	γραῦ	[βοῦ]
	Acc.	βασιλέ-ᾱ	γραῦ-ν	βοῦ-ν
	Gen.	βασιλέως (ε-ος)	γρᾱ-ός	βο-ός
	Dat.	βασιλεῖ (ε-ῐ)	γρᾱ-ί	βο-ί
Dual.	N. V. A.	βασιλέ-ε	γρᾶ-ε	βό-ε
	G. D.	βασιλέ-οιν	γρᾱ-οῖν	βο-οῖν
Plural.	N. V.	βασιλεῖς or -ῆς(ε-ες)	γρᾶ-ες	βό-ες
	Acc.	βασιλέ-ας	γραῦ-ς (α-ας)	βοῦ-ς (ο-ας)
	Gen.	βασιλέ-ων	γρᾱ-ῶν	βο-ῶν
	Dat.	βασιλεῦ-σι(ν)	γραυ-σί(ν)	βου-σί(ν)

The stems in ευ are all masculine.

Stems in αυ and ου lose the υ of the stem before vowel case-endings.

XXIV.—Stems in ο and ω.

πειθο, f. *persuasion*; αἰδο, f. *shame*; ἡρω, m. *hero*.

Singular.	Nom.	πειθώ	αἰδώς	ἥρω-ς
	Voc.	πειθοῖ	αἰδοῖ	ἥρω-ς
	Acc.	πειθώ (ό-α)	αἰδώ (ό-α)	ἥρω-α, ἥρω
	Gen.	πειθοῦς (ό-ος)	αἰδοῦς (ό-ος)	ἥρω-ος
	Dat.	πειθοῖ (ό-ϊ)	αἰδοῖ (ό-ϊ)	ἥρω-ϊ
Dual.	N. V. A.	When used, are like Second Declension.		ἥρω-ε
	G. D.			ἡρώ-οιν
Plural.	N. V.			ἥρω-ες
	Acc.			ἥρω-ας
	Gen.			ἡρώ-ων
	Dat.			ἥρω-σι(ν)

ELIDED STEMS,

or Stems that reject their final consonant in certain forms.

XXV.—Stems which elide ς.

Δημοσθενες, m. *Demosthenes* ; γενες, n. *race.*

Singular.	Nom.	Δημοσθένης	γένος
	Voc.	Δημόσθενες	γένος
	Acc.	Δημοσθένη (ε-α)	γένος
	Gen.	Δημοσθένους (ε-ος)	γένους (ε-ος)
	Dat.	Δημοσθένει (ε-ϊ)	γένει (ε-ϊ)
Dual.	N. V. A.		γένη (ε-ε)
	G. D.		γενοῖν (ε-οιν)
Plural.	N. V. A.		γένη (ε-α)
	Gen.		γενῶν (έ-ων)
	Dat.		γένε-σι(ν)

The stem γενες would form its Gen., γένεσ-ος (cp. *gener-is*). The σ was elided and γένε-ος contracted to -γένους. *So with the other cases.*

XXVI.—Stems which elide τ.

κεράτ, n. *horn* ; κρεάτ, n. *meat.*

Singular.	N. V. A.	κέρᾰς	κρέας
	Gen.	κέρᾱτ-ος, κέρως	κρέως (ατ-ος)
	Dat.	κέρᾱτ-ι, κέρᾳ	κρέᾳ (ατ-ι)
Dual.	N. V. A.	κέρᾱτ-ε, κέρᾱ	
	G. D.	κεράτ-οιν, κερῷν	
Plural.	N. V. A.	κέρᾱτ-α, κέρᾱ	κρέᾰ (ατ-α)
	Gen.	κεράτ-ων, κερῶν	κρεῶν (ατ-ων)
	Dat.	κέρᾰ-σι(ν)	κρέᾰ-σι(ν)

These stems are all Neuter.

τ becomes ς in the Nom. Acc. Voc. Sing. In the other cases some words always reject τ, as κρέας.

XXVII.—Several neuter stems in αρτ throw out τ in the Nom., Acc., and Voc. Sing., and ρ in the other cases, as, φρέαρ, *well*, Gen. φρέᾱτ-ος (st. φρεαρτ); ἧπαρ, *liver*, Gen. ἥπᾰτ-ος (st. ἡπαρτ); ἄλειφαρ, *salve*, Gen. ἀλείφᾰτ-ος (st. ἀλειφαρτ). Similarly, σκώρ, *dirt*, Gen. σκᾰτ-ός (st. σκαρτ); ὕδωρ, *water*, Gen. ὕδᾰτ-ος (st. ὑδαρτ).

XXVIII.—Some nouns take forms from two declensions. Thus proper names like Δημοσθένης above have more commonly the Acc. in -ην, as if from First Declension. But proper names in -κλῆς follow the Third Declension throughout.

XXIX.—OTHER IRREGULAR FORMS IN ALPHABETICAL ORDER.

	Stem.	ἀνερ, m.	γαλακτ, n.	γονᾰτ, n.	γυναικ, f.
	English.	*man.*	*milk.*	*knee.*	*woman.*
Singular.	Nom.	ἀνήρ	γάλα	γόνυ	γυνή
	Voc.	ἄνερ	γάλα	γόνυ	γύναι
	Acc.	ἄν-δ-ρ-ᾰ	γάλα	γόνυ	γυναῖκ-ᾰ
	Gen.	ἀν-δ-ρ-ός	γάλακτ-ος	γόνᾰτ-ος	γυναικ-ός
	Dat.	ἀν-δ-ρ-ῐ́	γάλακτ-ῐ	γόνᾰτ-ῐ	γυναικ-ῐ́
Dual.	N. V. A.	ἄν-δ-ρ-ε		γόνᾰτ-ε	γυναῖκ-ε
	G. D.	ἀν-δ-ρ-οῖν		γονά̆τ-οιν	γυναικ-οῖν
Plural.	N. V.	ἄν-δ-ρ-ες	γάλακτ-ᾰ	γόνᾰτ-ᾰ	γυναῖκ-ες
	Acc.	ἄν-δ-ρ-ᾰς	γάλακτ-ᾰ	γόνᾰτ-α	γυναῖκ-ᾰς
	Gen.	ἀν-δ-ρ-ῶν	γαλάκτ-ων	γονά̆τ-ων	γυναικ-ῶν
	Dat.	ἀν-δ-ρά̆-σι(ν)	γάλαξι(ν)	γόνᾰ-σι(ν)	γυναιξί(ν)

	Stem.	δορᾰτ, n.	ἐαρ, and ἠρ, n.	Ζευ, Δῐ, m.	κλειδ, f.	κυον and κυν, m. and f.
	English.	*spear.*	*spring.*	*Zeus.*	*key.*	*dog.*
Singular.	Nom.	δόρυ	ἔαρ	Ζεύ-ς	κλεί-ς	κύων
	Voc.	δόρυ	ἔαρ	Ζεῦ	κλεί-ς	κύον
	Acc.	δόρυ	ἔαρ	Δί-α	κλεῖ-ν	κύν-α
	Gen.	δόρᾰτ-ος, δορός	ἦρ-ος	Δι-ός	κλειδ-ός	κῠν-ός
	Dat.	δόρᾰτ-ι, δορί, or δόρει	ἦρ-ῑ	Δι-ί	κλειδ-ί	κῠν-ί
Dual.	N. A.V.	δόρᾰτ-ε			κλεῖδ-ε	κύν-ε
	G. D.	δορά̆τ-οιν			κλειδ--οῖν	κῠν-οῖν
Plural.	N. V.	δόρᾰτ-ᾰ			κλεῖδ-ες, κλεῖς	κύν-ες
	Acc.	δόρᾰτ-ᾰ			κλεῖδ-ᾰς, κλεῖς	κύν-ας
	Gen.	δοράτ-ων			κλειδ-ῶν	κῠν-ῶν
	Dat.	δόρᾰ-σι(ν)			κλει-σί(ν)	κυ-σί(ν)

OTHER IRREGULAR FORMS IN ALPHABETICAL ORDER—*continued.*

Stem.		μαρτυ, μαρτυρ, m. f.	ναυ, f.	ὀρνῑθ, ὀρνῐ, m. f.	ὠτ, n.
English.		*witness.*	*ship.*	*bird.*	*ear.*
Singular.	Nom.	μάρτυ-ς	ναῦ-ς	ὄρνῐ-ς	οὖ-ς
	Voc.	μάρτυ-ς		ὄρνι	οὖ-ς
	Acc.	μάρτῠρ-α	ναῦ-ν	ὄρνῑθᾰ, ὄρνι-ν	οὖ-ς
	Gen.	μάρτῠρ-ος	νε-ώς	ὄρνῑθ-ος	ὠτ-ός
	Dat.	μάρτῠρ-ι	νη-ΐ	ὄρνιθ-ῐ	ὠτ-ΐ
Dual.	N. A. V.	μάρτῠρ-ε		ὄρνῑθ-ε	ὦτ-ε
	G. D.	μαρτῠ́ρ-οιν	νε-οῖν	ὀρνίθ-οιν	ὠτ-οῖν
Plural.	N. V.	μάρτῠρ-ες	νῆ-ες	ὄρνῑθ-ες, ὄρνεις	ὦτ-ᾰ
	Acc.	μάρτῠρ-ας	ναῦς	ὄρνῑθ-ᾰς, ὄρνεις	ὦτ-ᾰ
	Gen.	μαρτῠ́ρ-ων	νε-ῶν	ὀρνίθ-ων, ὀρνέ-ων	ὤτ-ων
	Dat.	μάρτυ-σι(ν)	ναυ-σί(ν)	ὄρνῑ-σι(ν)	ὠ-σί(ν)

OTHER IRREGULAR FORMS IN ALPHABETICAL ORDER.—*continued.*

	Stem.	ποδ, m.	πυρ, πυρο, n.	υἱο, υἱευ, m.		χειρ, χερ, f.
	English.	*foot.*	*fire*, pl. = *watch-fires.*	*son.*		*hand.*
Singular.	Nom.	πού-ς	πῦρ	υἱό-ς		χείρ
	Voc.	πού-ς	πῦρ	υἱέ		χείρ
	Acc.	πόδ-ἄ	πῦρ	υἱό-ν		χεῖρ-ἄ
	Gen.	ποδ-ός	πυρ-ός	υἱοῦ	υἱέ-ος	χειρ-ός
	Dat.	ποδ-ΐ	πυρ-ΐ	υἱῷ	υἱεῖ (έ-ϊ)	χειρ-ΐ
Dual.	N. A.V.	πόδ-ε			υἱέ-ε	χεῖρ-ε
	G. D.	ποδ-οῖν			υἱέ-οιν	χερ-οῖν
Plural.	N. V.	πόδ-ες	πυρά	υἱοί	υἱεῖς (έ-ες)	χεῖρ-ες
	Acc.	πόδ-ἄς	πυρά	υἱούς	υἱεῖς (έα-ς)	χεῖρ-ας
	Gen.	ποδ-ῶν	πυρῶν	υἱῶν	υἱέ-ων	χειρ-ῶν
	Dat.	πο-σί(ν)	πυροῖς	υἱοῖς	υἱέ-σι(ν)	χερ-σί(ν)

DECLENSION OF ADJECTIVES.

ADJECTIVES OF THE FIRST AND SECOND DECLENSION.

XXX.—SIMPLE.

ἀγαθός, *good*; φίλιος, *friendly*.

		MASC.	FEM.	NEUT.	MASC.	FEM.	NEUT.
Singular.	Nom.	ἀγαθός	ἀγαθή	ἀγαθόν	φίλιος	φιλίᾱ	φίλιον
	Voc.	ἀγαθέ	ἀγαθή	ἀγαθόν	φίλιε	φιλίᾱ	φίλιον
	Acc.	ἀγαθόν	ἀγαθήν	ἀγαθόν	φίλιον	φιλίᾱν	φίλιον
	Gen.	ἀγαθοῦ	ἀγαθῆς	ἀγαθοῦ	φιλίου	φιλίᾱς	φιλίου
	Dat.	ἀγαθῷ	ἀγαθῇ	ἀγαθῷ	φιλίῳ	φιλίᾳ	φιλίῳ
Dual.	N.V.A.	ἀγαθώ	ἀγαθά	ἀγαθώ	φιλίω	φιλίᾱ	φιλίω
	G. D.	ἀγαθοῖν	ἀγαθαῖν	ἀγαθοῖν	φιλίοιν	φιλίαιν	φιλίοιν
Plural.	N. V.	ἀγαθοί	ἀγαθαί	ἀγαθά	φίλιοι	φίλιαι	φίλιᾰ
	Acc.	ἀγαθούς	ἀγαθάς	ἀγαθά	φιλίους	φιλίᾱς	φίλιᾰ
	Gen.	ἀγαθῶν	ἀγαθῶν	ἀγαθῶν	φιλίων	φιλίων	φιλίων
	Dat.	ἀγαθοῖς	ἀγαθαῖς	ἀγαθοῖς	φιλίοις	φιλίαις	φιλίοις

Most adjectives belong to this class.

DECLENSION OF ADJECTIVES.

ADJECTIVES OF THE FIRST AND SECOND DECLENSION.

XXXI.—CONTRACTED.

χρύσεος, *golden*; ἁπλόος, *simple*.

		MASC.	FEM.	NEUT.	MASC.	FEM.	NEUT.
Singular.	Nom.	χρυσοῦς	χρυσῆ	χρυσοῦν	ἁπλοῦς	ἁπλῆ	ἁπλοῦν
	Voc.	χρυσοῦς	χρυσῆ	χρυσοῦν	ἁπλοῦς	ἁπλῆ	ἁπλοῦν
	Acc.	χρυσοῦν	χρυσῆν	χρυσοῦν	ἁπλοῦν	ἁπλῆν	ἁπλοῦν
	Gen.	χρυσοῦ	χρυσῆς	χρυσοῦ	ἁπλοῦ	ἁπλῆς	ἁπλοῦ
	Dat.	χρυσῷ	χρυσῇ	χρυσῷ	ἁπλῷ	ἁπλῇ	ἁπλῷ
Dual.	N.V. A.	χρυσώ	χρυσᾶ	χρυσώ	ἁπλώ	ἁπλᾶ	ἁπλώ
	G. D.	χρυσοῖν	χρυσαῖν	χρυσοῖν	ἁπλοῖν	ἁπλαῖν	ἁπλοῖν
Plural.	N. V.	χρυσοῖ	χρυσαῖ	χρυσᾶ	ἁπλοῖ	ἁπλαῖ	ἁπλᾶ
	Acc.	χρυσοῦς	χρυσᾶς	χρυσᾶ	ἁπλοῦς	ἁπλᾶς	ἁπλᾶ
	Gen.	χρυσῶν	χρυσῶν	χρυσῶν	ἁπλῶν	ἁπλῶν	ἁπλῶν
	Dat.	χρυσοῖς	χρυσαῖς	χρυσοῖς	ἁπλοῖς	ἁπλαῖς	ἁπλοῖς

Rule 1.—The Fem. Sing. of adjectives in -εος contracts to η when a consonant precedes, but to α when a vowel or ρ precedes, as: χρυσέα, χρυσῆ, but ἐρεέα (woollen), ἐρεᾶ, ἀργυρέα (silvery), ἀργυρᾶ.

Rule 2.—α in the Nom. Sing. is always long.

XXXII.—Many adjectives of this class have only two endings, -ος for the Masc. and Fem. -ον for the Neut. This is the case with all compound adjectives.

XXXIII.—A few adjectives in -ως follow the Attic Second Declension, as ἵλεως, ἵλεων, gracious.

ADJECTIVES OF THE THIRD DECLENSION.

XXXIV.—A. Some adjectives follow the Third Declension in the Masc. and Neut. and form a Fem. in the suffix -ια, which combines with the stem in various ways.

To this class belong all participles of the Active Voice and some of the Passive Voice. They have no distinctive form for the Voc. Sing., the Nom. being used when a Voc. is required.

Participle stems in -εντ differ from adjective stems of a like kind in one important point. Participle stems compensate in the usual way for dropping their final ντ before the σ of the Dat. Pl., adjective stems drop the consonants without compensation: st. χαριεντ (Nom. Sing. χαρίεις, *graceful*), Dat. Pl. χαρίεσι(ν), st. λυθεντ (Nom. Sing. λυθείς, *loosed*), Dat. Pl. λυθεῖσι(ν).

Singular.	Nom.	ἡδύς	ἡδεῖα	ἡδύ	μέλᾱς	μέλαινα	μέλᾰν
	Voc.	ἡδύς	ἡδεῖα	ἡδύ	μέλᾰν	μέλαινα	μέλᾰν
	Acc.	ἡδύν	ἡδεῖαν	ἡδύ	μέλᾰνα	μέλαιναν	μέλᾰν
	Gen.	ἡδέος	ἡδείας	ἡδέος	μέλᾰνος	μελαίνης	μέλᾰνος
	Dat.	ἡδεῖ	ἡδείᾳ	ἡδεῖ	μέλᾰνι	μελαίνῃ	μέλᾰνι
Dual.	N.V.A.	ἡδέε	ἡδείᾱ	ἡδέε	μέλᾰνε	μελαίνᾱ	μέλᾰνε
	G. D.	ἡδέοιν	ἡδείαιν	ἡδέοιν	μελᾰ́νοιν	μελαίναιν	μελᾰ́νοιν
Plural.	N. V.	ἡδεῖς	ἡδεῖαι	ἡδέα	μέλᾰνες	μέλαιναι	μέλᾰνα
	Acc.	ἡδεῖς	ἡδείας	ἡδέα	μέλᾰνᾱς	μελαίνᾱς	μέλᾰνα
	Gen.	ἡδέων	ἡδειῶν	ἡδέων	μελᾰ́νων	μελαινῶν	μελᾰ́νων
	Dat.	ἡδέσι(ν)	ἡδείαις	ἡδέσι(ν)	μέλᾰσι(ν)	μελαίναις	μέλᾰσι(ν)

Adj. like μέλας may have the Voc. the same as the Nom. Like μέλας is also declined τέρην, τέρεινα, τέρεν, *tender*.

XXXV.—Stems in -εντ, -οντ, -αντ, and -υντ.

Sing. { N. V. λυθείς, λυθεῖσα, λυθέν, *loosed.*
Acc. λυθέντα, λυθεῖσαν, λυθέν.
&c. &c. }

Pl. Dat. λυθεῖσι(ν), λυθείσαις, λυθεῖσι(ν)

So all participles in st. -εντ.

Sing. { Nom. χαρίεις, χαρίεσσα, χαρίεν, *graceful.*
Voc. χαρίεν, χαρίεσσα, χαρίεν.
Acc. χαρίεντα, χαρίεσσαν, χαρίεν. }

Pl. Dat. χαρίεσι(ν), χαριέσσαις, χαρίεσι(ν).

So all adjectives in st. -εντ.

Sing. { N. V. λύων, λύουσᾰ, λῦον, *loosing.*
Acc. λύοντα, λύουσᾰν, λῦον. }

Pl. Dat. λύουσι(ν), λυούσαις, λύουσι(ν).

So are declined all participles in -ων (uncontracted).

Sing. { N. V. διδούς, διδοῦσα, διδόν, *offering.*
Acc. διδόντα, διδοῦσαν, διδόν. }

Pl. Dat. διδοῦσι(ν), διδούσαις, διδοῦσι(ν).

So are declined all participles in -ους.

Sing. { N. V. λύσᾱς, λύσᾱσᾰ, λῦσᾰν, *loosing.*
Acc. λύσαντα, λύσᾱσαν, λῦσᾰν. }

Pl. Dat. λύσᾱσι(ν), λυσάσαις, λύσᾱσι(ν).

So are declined all participles in st. -αντ.

Sing. { N. V. δεικνύς, δεικνῦσα, δεικνύν, *showing.*
Acc. δεικνύντα, δεικνῦσαν, δεικνύν. }

Pl. Dat. δεικνῦσι(ν), δεικνύσαις, δεικνῦσι(ν).

So are declined all participles in st. -υντ.

XXXVI.—Stems in -οτ.

Sing. { N. V. λελυκώς, λελυκυῖα, λελυκός, *having loosed.*
Acc. λελὔκότα, λελυκυῖαν, λελὔκός.

Pl. Dat. λελυκόσι(ν) λελυκυίαις, λελυκόσι(ν).

So are declined all participles in st. -οτ.

XXXVII.—B. Some adjectives follow the Third Declension entirely, having only two terminations.

εὐγενής (m. and f.), εὐγενές (neut.), *well-born* (st. εὐγενεσ).

Singular.	N. V.	εὐγενής	εὐγενές
	Acc.	εὐγενῆ (ε-α)	εὐγενές
	Gen.	εὐγενοῦς (ε-ος)	
	Dat.	εὐγενεῖ (ε-ϊ)	
Dual.	N. V. A.	εὐγενῆ (ε-ε)	
	G. D.	εὐγενοῖν (ε-οιν)	
Plural.	N. V.	εὐγενεῖς (ε-ες)	εὐγενῆ (ε-α)
	Acc.	εὐγενεῖς (ε-ας)	εὐγενῆ (ε-α)
	Gen.	εὐγενῶν (ε-ων)	
	Dat.	εὐγενέ-σι(ν)	

The pupil should re-read § XXV. above.

εὔφρων (m. and f.), **εὔφρον** (neut.), ***kindly***, (st. **εὐφρον**).
μείζων (m. and f.), **μεῖζον** (neut.), *greater*, (st. **μειζον**).

Singular.	N. V.	εὔφρων	εὔφρον	μείζων	μεῖζον
	Acc.	εὔφρον-α	εὔφρον	μείζον-α, μείζω	μεῖζον
	Gen.	εὔφρον-ος		μείζον-ος	
	Dat.	εὔφρον-ι		μείζον-ι	
Dual.	N.V.A.	εὔφρον-ε		μείζον-ε	
	G. D.	εὐφρόν-οιν		μειζόν-οιν	
Plural.	N. V.	εὔφρον-ες	εὔφρον-α	μείζον-ες, μείζους	μείζον-α, μείζω
	Acc.	εὔφρον-ας	εὔφρον-α	μείζον-ας, μείζους	μείζον-α, μείζω
	Gen.	εὐφρόν-ων		μειζόν-ων	
	Dat.	εὔφρο-σι(ν)		μείζο-σι(ν)	

Only comparative stems, like μειζον, elide ν and contract.

XXXVIII.—(C) Many adjectives have only one termination, the Neut. being alien to their meaning, or not compatible with their stem. Thus as there are no Neut. substantives with a guttural stem, so the adjectives in guttural stems have no Neut. forms. ἧλιξ, *of the same age* (st. ἡλῐκ); ἅρπαξ, *rapacious* (st. ἁρπαγ).

XXXIX.—Irregular are μέγας, μεγάλη, μέγα, *great* (st. μεγα and μεγᾰλο); and πολύς, πολλή, πολύ, *much* (st. πολυ and πολλο).

	Singular.			*Singular.*		
N. V.	μέγας	μεγάλη	μέγα	πολύς	πολλή	πολύ
Acc.	μέγαν	μεγάλην	μέγα	πολύν	πολλήν	πολύ
Gen.	μεγάλου	μεγάλης	μεγάλου	πολλοῦ	πολλῆς	πολλοῦ
Dat.	μεγάλῳ	μεγάλῃ	μεγάλῳ	πολλῷ	πολλῇ	πολλῷ
	Dual.					
N.V.A.	μεγάλω	μεγάλᾱ	μεγάλω	No Dual.		
G. D.	μεγάλοιν	μεγάλαιν	μεγάλοιν			
	Plural.			*Plural.*		
N. V.	μεγάλοι	μεγάλαι	μεγάλᾰ	πολλοί	πολλαί	πολλά
Acc.	μεγάλους	μεγάλᾱς	μεγάλᾰ	πολλούς	πολλάς	πολλά
Gen.	μεγάλων	μεγάλων	μεγάλων	πολλῶν	πολλῶν	πολλῶν
Dat.	μεγάλοις	μεγάλαις	μεγάλοις	πολλοῖς	πολλαῖς	πολλοῖς

XL.—COMPARISON OF ADJECTIVES.

(1) The most common method is to add to the stem the suffix *-τερος*, *-τερα*, *-τερον* to form the comparative, and *-τατος*, *-τάτη*, *-τατον* to form the superlative degree. In *-ο* stems the stem-vowel is lengthened to *ω*, if the preceding syllable is short or common.

Positive.	Stem.	Comparative.	Superlative.
κοῦφος, *light*	κουφο	κουφό-τερος	κουφό-τατος
γλυκύς, *sweet*	γλυκυ	γλυκύ-τερος	γλυκύ-τατος
μέλας, *black*	μελαν	μελάν-τερος	μελάν-τατος
χαρίεις, *graceful*	χαριεντ	χαριέσ-τερος	χαριέσ-τατος
σαφής, *clear*	σαφες	σαφέσ-τερος	σαφέσ-τατος
μάκαρ, *happy*	μακαρ	μακάρ-τερος	μακάρ-τατος
σοφός, *wise*	σοφο	σοφώ-τερος	σοφώ-τατος

Some stems in *-αιο* drop the *ο*, as:

γεραιός, *aged*, γεραιο γεραί-τερος γεραί-τατος.

Some other stems change *ο* into *αι*, as:

μέσος, *middle*, μεσο μεσαί-τερος μεσαί-τατος.
ἴσος, *equal*, ἰσο ἰσαί-τερος ἰσαί-τατος.
εὔδιος, *calm*, εὐδιο εὐδιαί-τερος εὐδιαί-τατος.

Φίλος sometimes drops the *ο*, as φίλ-τερος, φίλ-τατος.

XLI.—Stems in -*ον*, and some others, have -*έστερος* and -*έστατος*. Final *ο* is dropped.

Positive.	Stem.	Comparative.	Superlative.
σώφρων, *prudent*	σωφρον	σωφρον-έστερος	σωφρον-έστατος
ἀφῆλιξ, *aged*	ἀφηλικ	ἀφηλικ-έστερος	ἀφηλικ-έστατος
εὔνους, *kindly*	εὐνοο	εὐνούστερος (for εὐνο-έστερος)	εὐνούστατος (for εὐνο-έστατος)
ἄκρᾱτος, *unmixed*	ἀκρατο	ἀκρατ-έστερος	ἀκρατ-έστατος

A few add -*ίστερος*, -*ίστατος*, dropping the vowel, as:

λάλος, *talkative* (λαλο), λαλ-ίστερος, λαλ-ίστατος.
πτωχός, *beggarly* (πτωχο), πτωχ-ίστερος, πτωχ-ίστατος.
κλέπτης, *thievish* (κλεπτα), κλεπτ-ίστερος, κλεπτ-ίστατος

XLII.—(2) The second and rarer ending is -*ιων* for comparatives, -*ιστος* for superlatives. The stem-vowel is dropped before both. For the inflexion of the comparatives, see § XXXVII.

Positive.	Stem.	Comparative.	Superlative.
ἡδύς, *sweet*	ἡδυ	ἡδ-ίων	ἥδ-ιστος
ταχύς, *swift*	ταχυ	θάσσων (for ταχ-ιων)	τάχ-ιστος
μέγας, *great*	μεγα	μείζων (for μεγ-ιων)	μέγ-ιστος
ἐχθρός, *hostile*	ἐχθρο	ἐχθ-ίων	ἔχθ-ιστος
αἰσχρός, *base*	αἰσχρο	αἰσχ-ίων	αἴσχ-ιστος

Observe that stems in -ρο lose ρ.

XLIII.—IRREGULAR COMPARISON.

Positive.	Comparative.	Superlative.
ἀγᾰθός, *good*	—	—
	ἀμείνων	—
	—	ἄριστος
	βελτίων	βέλτιστος
	κρείσσων (*superior*)	κράτιστος
κακός, *bad*	κακίων	κάκιστος
	χείρων (*deterior*)	χείριστος (*deterrimus*)
	.ἥσσων (*inferior*)	ἥκιστα N. Pl. as Adv.
μικρός, *small*	μικρότερος	μικρότατος
	μείων	—
ὀλίγος, *little*	—	ὀλίγιστος
	ἐλάσσων	ἐλάχιστος
πολύς, *much*	πλείων or πλέων	πλεῖστος
κᾰλός, *beautiful*	καλλίων	κάλλιστος
ῥᾴδιος, *easy*	ῥᾴων	ῥᾷστος
ἀλγεινός, *painful*	ἀλγίων	ἄλγιστος
(πρό, *before*)	πρότερος (*prior*)	πρῶτος (*primus*)
(πέραν, *on the other side*)	περαίτερος	—

XLIV.—ADVERBS.

Adverbs are derived from adjectives by affixing -ως to the stem. Stems in ο drop this vowel: φίλο-ς, adv. φίλ-ως. In stems of the Third Declension, the -ως is affixed to that form of the stem which occurs in the Gen. Sing., ταχύ-ς, Gen. ταχέ-ος, *swift*; adv. ταχέ-ως; σαφής, Gen. σαφέ-ος, *clear*; adv. σαφέ-ως, contracted σαφῶς. Contraction occurs only when the Gen. also is contracted.

XLV.—COMPARISON OF ADVERBS. As a rule the Comparative of an Adverb is the Neut. Acc. Sing. of the Comparative of the Adjective, and its Superlative the Neut. Acc. Pl. of the Superlative of the Adjective, as:

σοφῶς, *wisely*, σοφώτερον, *more wisely*, σοφώτατα, *most wisely*.

XLVI.—NUMERALS. The first four Cardinal Numerals are declined: εἷς, *one*; δύο, *two*; τρεῖς, *three*; τέσσαρες, *four*.

Nom.	εἷ-ς μία ἕν	N. A. δύο
Acc.	ἕν-α μίαν ἕν	
Gen.	ἑν-ός μιᾶς ἑν-ός	G. D. δυοῖν
Dat.	ἑν-ί μιᾷ ἑν-ί	
Nom.	τρεῖς τρί-α	τέσσαρ-ες τέσσαρ-α
Acc.	τρεῖς τρί-α	τέσσαρ-ας τέσσαρ-α
Gen.	τρι-ῶν	τεσσάρ-ων
Dat.	τρι-σί(ν)	τέσσαρ-σι(ν)

Like εἷς are declined οὐδείς, οὐδεμία, οὐδέν, and μηδείς, μηδεμία, μηδέν, *no one*.

XLVII.—THE PRONOUNS.

THE PERSONAL PRONOUNS.

		I, me; we, us.	*Thou, thee; you.*	*He, she, it, him, her; they, them.*			
Singular.	Nom.	ἐγώ	σύ	—	—	—	—
	Voc.	—	σύ	—	—	—	—
	Acc.	ἐμέ, μέ	σέ	αὐτόν	αὐτήν	αὐτό	(ἕ)
	Gen.	ἐμοῦ, μοῦ	σοῦ	αὐτοῦ	αὐτῆς	αὐτοῦ	(οὗ)
	Dat.	ἐμοί, μοί	σοί	αὐτῷ	αὐτῇ	αὐτῷ	οἷ
Dual.	N. A.	νώ	σφώ	—	—	—	—
	G. D.	νῷν	σφῷν	αὐτοῖν	αὐταῖν	αὐτοῖν	—
Plural.	Nom.	ἡμεῖς	ὑμεῖς	—	—	—	σφεῖς
	Voc.	—	ὑμεῖς	—	—	—	—
	Acc.	ἡμᾶς	ὑμᾶς	αὐτούς	αὐτάς	αὐτά	σφᾶς
	Gen.	ἡμῶν	ὑμῶν	αὐτῶν	αὐτῶν	αὐτῶν	σφῶν
	Dat.	ἡμῖν	ὑμῖν	αὐτοῖς	αὐταῖς	αὐτοῖς	σφίσι(ν)

There is no true Personal Pronoun of the Third Person in Greek. The Nom. is expressed in various ways, the other cases as above.

XLVIII.—The Possessive Pronouns are, ἐμός, ἐμή, ἐμόν, *my, mine*; ἡμέτερος, α, ον, *our*; σός, σή, σόν, *thy, thine*; ὑμέτερος, α, ον, *your*. They are declined like adjectives, but σός and ὑμέτερος have no Voc.

XLIX.—αὐτός, αὐτή, αὐτό has the meaning *self* in the Nom. In the other cases it has this meaning, and also another meaning, *him, her, it*. It is declined like adjectives in -ος, except that the Neut. in the Nom. and Acc. Sing. has no ν.

L.—The principal Demonstrative Pronouns are ὅδε, ἥδε, τόδε, *this*; οὗτος, αὕτη, τοῦτο, *this*; and ἐκεῖνος, ἐκείνη, ἐκεῖνο, *that, yonder*. ὅδε is declined like the Definite Article, the suffix δε being added to each case. ἐκεῖνος is declined like αὐτός. The forms of οὗτος are :—

Singular.	Nom.	οὗτος	αὕτη	τοῦτο
	Acc.	τοῦτον	ταύτην	τοῦτο
	Gen.	τούτου	ταύτης	τούτου
	Dat.	τούτῳ	ταύτῃ	τούτῳ
Dual.	N. A.	τούτω	ταύτᾱ	τούτω
	G. D.	τούτοιν	ταύταιν	τούτοιν
Plural.	Nom.	οὗτοι	αὗται	ταῦτα
	Acc.	τούτους	ταύτας	ταῦτα
	Gen.	τούτων	τούτων	τούτων
	Dat.	τούτοις	ταύταις	τούτοις

LI.—The Reflexive Pronouns are :—

		Sing. *myself*, Pl. *ourselves.*	Sing. *thyself*, Pl. *yourselves.*	Sing. *himself*, *herself*, *itself*, Pl. *themselves.*
Singular.	Acc.	ἐμαυτόν, -ήν	σεαυτόν, -ήν	ἑαυτόν, -ήν, -ό
	Gen.	ἐμαυτοῦ, -ῆς	σεαυτοῦ, -ῆς	ἑαυτοῦ, -ῆς, -οῦ
	Dat.	ἐμαυτῷ, -ῇ	σεαυτῷ, -ῇ	ἑαυτῷ, -ῇ, -ῷ
Plural.	Acc.	ἡμᾶς αὐτούς, -άς	ὑμᾶς αὐτούς, -άς	ἑαυτούς, -άς, -ά
	Gen.	ἡμῶν αὐτῶν	ὑμῶν αὐτῶν	ἑαυτῶν
	Dat.	ἡμῖν αὐτοῖς, -αῖς	ὑμῖν αὐτοῖς, -αῖς	ἑαυτοῖς, -αῖς, -οῖς

σεαυτόν and ἑαυτόν have often their cases contracted to σαυτόν, αὑτόν, &c. For Plural ἑαυτόν has sometimes the forms :—

Acc. σφᾶς αὐτούς, -άς. Gen. σφῶν αὐτῶν.
Dat. σφίσιν αὐτοῖς, -αῖς.

LII.—The forms of the Reciprocal Pronoun *each other* are:—

Dual.	Acc.	ἀλλήλω	ἀλλήλα	ἀλλήλω
	G. D.	ἀλλήλοιν	ἀλλήλαιν	ἀλλήλοιν
Plural.	Acc.	ἀλλήλους	ἀλλήλας	ἀλλήλα
	Gen.	ἀλλήλων	ἀλλήλων	ἀλλήλων
	Dat.	ἀλλήλοις	ἀλλήλαις	ἀλλήλοις

LIII.—The forms of the Relative Pronoun are:—

	Singular.			*Dual.*			*Plural.*		
Nom.	ὅς	ἥ	ὅ	ὥ	ἅ	ὥ	οἵ	αἵ	ἅ
Acc.	ὅν	ἥν	ὅ				οὕς	ἅς	ἅ
Gen.	οὗ	ἧς	οὗ	οἷν	αἷν	οἷν	ὧν	ὧν	ὧν
Dat.	ᾧ	ᾗ	ᾧ				οἷς	αἷς	οἷς

LIV.—The Interrogative Pronoun has the same stem as the Indefinite Pronoun, from which it is distinguished only by the accent. Interrogative: τίς, M. and F.; τί, N. Indefinite, τις, M. and F.; τι, N.

Singular.	Nom.	τίς	τί	τις	τι
	Acc.	τίνα	τί	τινά	τι
	Gen.	τίνος or τοῦ		τινός or του	
	Dat.	τίνι or τῷ		τινί or τῳ	
Dual.	N. A.	τίνε		τινέ	
	G. D.	τίνοιν		τινοῖν	
Plural.	Nom.	τίνες	τίνα	τινές	τινά or ἅττα
	Acc.	τίνας	τίνα	τινάς	τινά or ἅττα
	Gen.	τίνων		τινῶν	
	Dat.	τίσι(ν)		τισί(ν)	

The Relative Pronoun ὅς and the Indefinite Pronoun τις are declined together to form a Relative Pronoun ὅστις, ἥτις, ὅ τι, *whosoever, whatsoever*; Gen. οὗτινος, ἧστινος, οὗτινος.

THE VERB.

LV.—There are two Conjugations in Greek—Verbs in -ω, and Verbs in -μι.

The *Verb-stem* is that simple form which is modified to express relations of time and mood.

The Tenses, Moods, and Verbal Nouns are classified according to the Stems (*tense-stems*) from which they are derived.

LVI.—A complete Greek Verb has :—

(1) Three Numbers : Singular, Dual, and Plural.

Obs.—The Dual has no first person.

(2) Three Voices :—

Active, ἔλυσα, *I loosed.* Middle, ἐλυσάμην, *I loosed for myself.* Passive, ἐλύθην, *I was loosed.*

(3) Two classes of Tenses, *e.g.*—

Principal.

Present, λύω, *I loose.*
Future, λύσω, *I shall loose.*
Perfect, λέλυκα, *I have loosed.*

Historical.

Imperfect, ἔλυον, *I was loosing.*
Aorist, ἔλυσα, *I loosed.*
Pluperfect, ἐλελύκειν, *I had loosed.*

(4) Four Moods, *e.g.*—

Indicative, λύω, *I loose.*
Subjunctive, λύω, *I may loose.*
Optative, λύοιμι, *I would loose.*
Imperative, λῦε, *loose.*

(5) Three Verbal Nouns, *e.g.*—

Infinitive, λύειν, *to loose.* Participle, λύων, loosing. Verbal *Adjective*, λυτέος, *requiring to be loosed.*

I.—The following are the forms of the Verb εἶναι, *to be*. It belongs to the conjugation in -μι.

[TE]NSE.		INDICATIVE.		SUBJUNCTIVE.	OPTATIVE.	IMPERATIVE.		
		Present.	*Imperfect.*					
Present and Imperf.	S. 1.	εἰ-μί	ἦν or ἦ	ὦ	εἴην	—	εἶ-ναι	ὤν, οὖσα, ὄν stem, ὀντ.
	2.	εἶ	ἦσ-θα	ᾖ-ς	εἴης	ἴσ-θι		
	3.	ἐσ-τί(ν)	ἦν	ᾖ	εἴη	ἔσ-τω		
	D. 2.	ἐσ-τόν	ἦσ-τον, or ἦ-τον	ἦ-τον	εἴητον	ἔσ-τον		
	3.	ἐσ-τόν	ἤσ-την, or ἤ-την	ἦ-τον	εἰήτην	ἔσ-των		
	P. 1.	ἐσ-μέν	ἦ-μεν	ὦ-μεν	εἴημεν, or εἶμεν	—		
	2.	ἐσ-τέ	ἦσ-τε, or ἦ-τε	ἦ-τε	εἴητε	ἔσ-τε		
	3.	εἰ-σί(ν)	ἦσ-αν	ὦ-σι(ν)	εἴησαν, or εἶεν	ἔσ τωσαν, or ἔσ-των		
Future.	S. 1.	ἔσ-ομαι			ἐσ-οίμην		ἔσ-εσθαι	ἐσ-όμενος, η, ον
	2.	ἔσ-ει			ἔσ-οιο			
	3.	ἔσ-ται			ἔσ-οιτο			
	D. 2.	ἔσ-εσθον			ἔσ-οισθον			
	3.	ἔσ-εσθον			ἐσ-οίσθην			
	P. 1.	ἐσ-όμεθα			ἐσ-οίμεθα			
	2.	ἔσ-εσθε			ἔσ-οισθε			
	3.	ἔσ-ονται			ἔσ-οιντο			

VERBS IN Ω.

Verbs in -ω are classified according to the final letter of the Verb-stem in the same way as we arranged the substantives. Thus we can form at once two great groups, *e.g.*—

(1) Verbs whose Verb-stems end in a Vowel.

(2) Verbs whose Verb-stems end in a Consonant.

The former of these classes is much more simple than the latter. Consonant-stems are often so altered in the Present and Imperfect that you will not be able at first to assign them to their proper classes. The succeeding pages will give you examples of verbs in -ω arranged in groups of which the following is a synopsis.

I. Vowel-Stems.

Soft Vowels ι, υ, αυ, ευ, ου [uncontracted].
Hard Vowels α, ε, ο [contracted].

II. Consonant-Stems.

Guttural Mutes, κ, γ, χ.
Dental Mutes, τ, δ, θ.
Labial Mutes, π, β, φ.
Liquids and Nasals, λ, ρ, μ, ν.

Note.—The expressions *strong* and *weak* which you will find applied to tenses may be best explained by examples from English. Thus *bore, took, sunk*, are the *strong* past tenses of *bear, take, sink*; but *neared, baked, linked*, are the *weak* past tenses of *near, bake, link*.

VERBS IN Ω.

Vowel-Stems. I. Uncontracted.—Active Voice.

λύω, *I loose.* Verb-stem λῡ.

TENSES.		INDICATIVE. *Present.*	INDICATIVE. *Imperfect.*	SUBJUNCTIVE.	OPTATIVE.	IMPERATIVE.	INF.	PAR.
Present and Imperfect. Stem λῡ.	S. 1.	λύ-ω	ἔ-λῡ-ον	λύ-ω	λύ-οιμι	—	λύ-ειν	λύ-ων, λύ-ουσα, λῦ-ον st. λυοντ.
	2.	λύ-εις	ἔ-λῡ-ες	λύ-ῃς	λύ-οις	λῦ-ε		
	3.	λύ-ει	ἔ-λῡ-ε(ν)	λύ-ῃ	λύ-οι	λῡ-έτω		
	D. 2.	λύ-ετον	ἐ-λύ-ετον	λύ-ητον	λύ-οιτον	λύ-ετον		
	3.	λύ-ετον	ἐ-λῡ-έτην	λύ-ητον	λῡ-οίτην	λῡ-έτων		
	P. 1.	λύ-ομεν	ἐ-λύ-ομεν	λύ-ωμεν	λύ-οιμεν	—		
	2.	λύ-ετε	ἐ-λύ-ετε	λύ-ητε	λύ-οιτε	λύ-ετε		
	3.	λύ-ουσι(ν)	ἔ-λῡ-ον	λύ-ωσι(ν)	λύ-οιεν	λῡ-έτωσαν / λῡ-όντων		
Future. Stem λῡσ.	S. 1.	λύ-σ-ω			λύ-σ-οιμι		λύ-σ-ειν	λύ-σ-ων, λύ-σ-ουσα, λῦ-σ-ον st. λῡσοντ.
	2.	λύ-σ-εις			λύ-σ-οις			
	3.	λύ-σ-ει			λύ-σ-οι			
	D. 2.	λύ-σ-ετον			λύ-σ-οιτον			
	3.	λύ-σ-ετον			λῡ-σ-οίτην			
	P. 1.	λύ-σ-ομεν			λύ-σ-οιμεν			
	2.	λύ-σ-ετε			λύ-σ-οιτε			
	3.	λύ-σ-ουσι(ν)			λύ-σ-οιεν			

[TE]NSES.		INDICATIVE.		SUBJUNCTIVE.	OPTATIVE.	IMPERATIVE.	INF.	PAR.
Weak Aorist. Stem λῡσ.	S. 1.		ἔ-λῡ-σ-α	λῡ́-σ-ω	λῡ́-σ-αιμι	—	λῦ-σ-αι	λῡ́-σ-ας, λῡ́-σ-ᾱσα, λῦ-σαν st. λυσαντ.
	2.		ἔ-λῡ-σ-ας	λῡ́-σ-ῃς	λῡ́-σ-αις, -σ-ειας	λῦ-σ-ον		
	3.		ἔ-λῡ-σ-ε(ν)	λῡ́-σ-ῃ	λῡ́-σ-αι, -σ-ειε(ν)	λῡ-σ-άτω		
	D. 2.		ἐ-λῡ́-σ-ατον	λῡ́-σ-ητον	λῡ́-σ-αιτον	λῡ́-σ-ατον		
	3.		ἐ-λῡ-σ-άτην	λῡ́-σ-ητον	λῡ-σ-αίτην	λῡ-σ-άτων		
	P. 1.		ἐ-λῡ́-σ-αμεν	λῡ́-σ-ωμεν	λῡ́-σ-αιμεν	—		
	2.		ἐ-λῡ́-σ-ατε	λῡ́-σ-ητε	λῡ́-σ-αιτε	λῡ́-σ-ατε		
	3.		ἔ-λῡ-σ-αν	λῡ́-σ-ωσι(ν)	λῡ́-σ-αιεν, -σ-ειαν	λῡ-σ-άτωσαν, λῡ-σ-άντων		
		Perfect.	*Pluperfect.*					
Weak Perfect and Pluperfect Stem λελυκ.	S. 1.	λέ-λῠ-κ-α	ἐ-λε-λῠ́-κ-ειν	λε-λῠ́-κ-ω	λε-λῠ́-κ-οιμι	—	λε-λυ-κ-έναι	λε-λῠ-κώς, λε-λυ-κυῖα, λε-λυκός. st. λελυκοτ.
	2.	λέ-λῠ-κ-ας	ἐ-λε-λῠ́-κ-εις	λε-λῠ́-κ-ῃς	λε-λῠ́-κ-οις	λέ-λῠ-κ-ε		
	3.	λέ-λῠ-κ-ε(ν)	ἐ-λε-λῠ́-κ-ει	λε-λῠ́-κ-ῃ	λε-λῠ́-κ-οι	λε-λῠ-κ-έτω		
	D. 2.	λε-λῠ́-κ-ατον	ἐ-λε-λῠ́-κ-ειτον	λε-λῠ́-κ-ητον	λε-λῠ́-κ-οιτον	λε-λῠ́-κ-ετον		
	3.	λε-λῠ́-κ-ατον	ἐ-λε-λῠ-κ-είτην	λε-λῠ́-κ-ητον	λε-λῠ-κ-οίτην	λε-λῠ-κ-έτων		
	P. 1.	λε-λῠ́-κ-αμεν	ἐ-λε-λῠ́-κ-ειμεν	λε-λῠ́-κ-ωμεν	λε-λῠ́-κ-οιμεν	—		
	2.	λε-λῠ́-κ-ατε	ἐ-λε-λῠ́-κ-ειτε	λε-λῠ́-κ-ητε	λε-λῠ́-κ-οιτε	λε-λῠ́-κ-ετε		
	3	λε-λῠ́-κ-ᾱσι(ν)	ἐ-λε-λῠ́-κ-εσαν	λε-λῠ́-κ-ωσι(ν)	λε-λῠ́-κ-οιεν	λε-λῠ-κ-έτωσαν, λε-λῠ-κ-όντων		
Strong Aorist.	Wanting in Vowel-stems. Has the same endings as Imperfect in Indicative and as the Present in other Moods.							
Strong Perf. and Plupf.	Wanting in Vowel-stems. Have the same endings as Weak Perfect and Pluperfect respectively.							

VERBS IN Ω.

Vowel-Stems. I. Uncontracted.—Middle Voice.

λύομαι, *I loose myself*, or *for myself.*

TENSES.		INDICATIVE. Present.	INDICATIVE. Imperfect.	SUBJUNCTIVE.	OPTATIVE.	IMPERATIVE.	INF.	PAR.
Present and Imperfect. Stem λῡ.	S. 1.	λύ-ομαι	ἐ-λῡ-όμην	λύ-ωμαι	λῡ-οίμην	—	λύ-εσθαι	λῡ-όμενος, η, ον.
	2.	λύ-ει, λύ-ῃ	ἐ-λύ-ου	λύ-ῃ	λύ-οιο	λύ-ου		
	3.	λύ-εται	ἐ-λύ-ετο	λύ-ηται	λύ-οιτο	λῡ-έσθω		
	D. 2.	λύ-εσθον	ἐ-λύ-εσθον	λύ-ησθον	λύ-οισθον	λύ-εσθον		
	3.	λύ-εσθον	ἐ-λῡ-έσθην	λύ-ησθον	λῡ-οίσθην	λῡ-έσθων		
	P. 1.	λῡ-όμεθα	ἐ-λῡ-όμεθα	λῡ-ώμεθα	λῡ-οίμεθα	—		
	2.	λύ-εσθε	ἐ-λύ-εσθε	λύ-ησθε	λύ-οισθε	λύ-εσθε		
	3.	λύ-ονται	ἐ-λύ-οντο	λύ-ωνται	λύ-οιντο	λῡ-έσθωσαν or λῡ-έσθων		
Future. Stem λῡσ.	S. 1.	λύ-σ-ομαι			λῡ-σ-οίμην		λύ-σ-εσθαι	λῡ-σ-όμενος, η, ον.
	2.	λύ-σ-ει, λύ-σ-ῃ			λύ-σ-οιο			
	3.	λύ-σ-εται			λύ-σ-οιτο			
	D. 2.	λύ-σ-εσθον			λύ-σ-οισθον			
	3.	λύ-σ-εσθον			λῡ-σ-οίσθην			
	P. 1.	λῡ-σ-όμεθον			λῡ-σ-οίμεθα			
	2.	λύ-σ-εσθε			λύ-σ-οισθε			
	3.	λύ-σ-ονται			λύ-σ-οιντο			

TENSES.		INDICATIVE.		SUBJUNCTIVE.	OPTATIVE.	IMPERATIVE.	INF.	PAR.
Weak Aorist. Stem λῡσ.	S. 1.		ἐ-λῡ-σ-άμην	λύ-σ-ωμαι	λῡ-σ-αίμην	—	λύ-σ-ασθαι	λῡ-σ-άμενος, η, ον.
	2.		ἐ-λύ-σ-ω	λύ-σ-ῃ	λύ-σ-αιο	λῦ-σ-αι		
	3.		ἐ-λύ-σ-ατο	λύ-σ-ηται	λύ-σ-αιτο	λῡ-σ-άσθω		
	D. 2.		ἐ-λύ-σ-ασθον	λύ-σ-ησθον	λύ-σ-αισθον	λύ-σ-ασθον		
	3.		ἐ-λῡ-σ-άσθην	λύ-σ-ησθον	λῡ-σ-αίσθην	λῡ-σ-άσθων		
	P. 1.		ἐ-λῡ-σ-άμεθα	λῡ-σ-ώμεθα	λῡ-σ-αίμεθα	—		
	2.		ἐ-λύ-σ-ασθε	λύ-σ-ησθε	λύ-σ-αισθε	λύ-σ-ασθε		
	3.		ἐ-λύ-σ-αντο	λύ-σ-ωνται	λύ-σ-αιντο	λῡ-σ-άσθωσαν or λῡ-σ-άσθων		
Perfect and Pluperfect Stem λελῠ.		*Perfect.*	*Pluperfect.*					
	S. 1.	λέ-λῠ-μαι	ἐ-λε-λύ-μην	λε-λῠ-μένος ὦ	λε-λῠ-μένος εἴην	—	λε-λύ-σθαι	λε-λῠ-μένος, η, ον.
	2.	λέ-λῠ-σαι	ἐ-λέ-λῠ-σο	ᾖς	εἴης	λέ-λῠ-σο		
	3.	λέ-λῠ-ται	ἐ-λέ-λῠ-το	ᾖ	εἴη	λε-λύ-σθω		
	D. 2.	λέ-λυ-σθον	ἐ-λέ-λυ-σθον	λε-λῠ-μένω ἦτον	λε-λῠ-μένω εἴητον	λέ-λυ-σθον		
	3.	λέ-λυ-σθον	ἐ-λε-λύ-σθην	ἦτον	εἰήτην	λε-λύ-σθων		
	P. 1.	λε-λύ-μεθα	ἐ-λε-λύ-μεθα	λε-λῠ-μένοι ὦμεν	λε-λῠ-μένοι εἴημεν	—		
	2.	λέ-λυ-σθε	ἐ-λέ-λυ-σθε	ἦτε	εἴητε	λέ-λυ-σθε		
	3.	λέ-λυ-νται	ἐ-λέ-λυ-ντο	ὦσι(ν)	εἴησαν	λε-λύ-σθωσαν or λε-λύ-σθων		
Future perfect. Stem λελῡσ.		λε-λύ-σ-ομαι λε-λύ-σ-ει, ῃ λε-λύ-σ-εται &c. as Present			λε-λῡ-σ-οίμην λε-λύ-σ-οιο λε-λύ-σ-οιτο &c. as Present		λε-λύ-σ-εσθαι	λε-λῡ-σ-όμενος
Strong Perf.		Wanting in Vowel-Stems.						

VOWEL-STEMS. I. Uncontracted. PASSIVE VOICE.

Identical with the Middle except in Aorist and Tenses derived from Aorist.

λύομαι, *I am loosed.*

TENSES.		INDICATIVE.	SUBJUNCTIVE.	OPTATIVE.	IMPERATIVE.	INF.	PARTC.
Weak Aorist. Stem λῠθ.	S. 1.	ἐ-λῠ-θ-ην	λῠ-θ-ῶ	λῠ-θ-είην		λῠ-θ-ῆναι	λῠ-θ-είς, εῖσα, έν. stem, λῠ-θ-εντ.
	2.	ἐ-λῠ-θ-ης	λῠ-θ-ῇς	λῠ-θ-είης	λῠ-θ-ητι		
	3.	ἐ-λῠ-θ-η	λῠ-θ-ῇ	λῠ-θ-είη	λῠ-θ-ήτω		
	D. 2.	ἐ-λῠ-θ-ητον	λῠ-θ-ῆτον	λῠ-θ-είητον, εῖτον	λῠ-θ-ητον		
	3.	ἐ-λῠ-θ-ήτην	λῠ-θ-ῆτον	λῠ-θ-ειήτην, είτην	λῠ-θ-ήτων		
	P. 1.	ἐ-λῠ-θ-ημεν	λῠ-θ-ῶμεν	λῠ-θ-είημεν, εῖμεν	—		
	2.	ἐ-λῠ-θ-ητε	λῠ-θ-ῆτε	λῠ-θ-είητε, εῖτε	λῠ-θ-ητε		
	3.	ἐ-λῠ-θ-ησαν	λῠ-θ-ῶσι(ν)	λῠ-θ-είησαν, εῖεν	λῠ-θ-ήτωσαν or λῠ-θ-έντων		
Weak Future. Stem λῠθησ.	S. 1.	λῠ-θήσ-ομαι		λῠ-θησ-οίμην		λῠ-θήσ-εσθαι	λῠ-θησ-όμενος, η, ον.
	2.	λῠ-θήσ-ει, ῃ		λῠ-θήσ-οιο			
	3.	λῠ-θήσ-εται		λῠ-θήσ-οιτο			
	D. 2.	λῠ-θήσ-εσθον		λῠ-θήσ-οισθον			
	3.	λῠ-θήσ-εσθον		λῠ-θησ-οίσθην			
	P. 1.	λῠ-θησ-όμεθον		λῠ-θησ-οίμεθα			
	2.	λῠ-θήσ-εσθε		λῠ-θήσ-οισθε			
	3.	λῠ-θήσ-ονται		λῠ-θήσ-οιντο			
Strong Aorist.		Wanting in Vowel-stems.	Has the same endings as Weak Aorist.				
Strong Future.		Wanting in Vowel-stems.	Has the same endings as Weak Future.				

Verbal Adjectives. { λῠ-τός, λυ-τή, λυ-τόν, *able, or fit, to be loosed.* / λῠ-τέος, λυ-τέα, λυ-τέον, *necessary to be loosed.* }

Obs.—The termination of the 2nd Pers. Sing. Imperative of the Strong Aor. Pass. is -θι.

THE AUGMENT.

The ε which is prefixed in the Historical Tenses of the Indicative Mood of λύω is called the Augment. All verbs beginning in a consonant have an augment of this form. It is called the Syllabic Augment.

When a verb begins with a vowel, the vowel is lengthened in the Historical Tenses of the Indicative Mood. Thus

α	becomes	η	ῐ	becomes	ῑ	αυ	becomes	ηυ
ε	„	η	ῠ	„	ῡ	οι	„	ῳ
	„	ω	αι	„	ῃ			

This is called the Temporal Augment.

η, ω, ῑ, ῡ and ει, ευ, ου, remain without Augment.

E 2

VERBS IN Ω.

VOWEL-STEMS. II. Contracted.

		τιμάω, άομαι, contracted τιμῶ, ῶμαι, *I honour.*		ποιέω, έομαι, con. ποιῶ, οῦμαι, *I make.*		δηλόω, όομαι, con. δηλῶ, οῦμαι, *I show.*	
		ACTIVE.	PASS. AND MID.	ACT.	PASS. AND MID.	ACT.	PASS. AND MID.
Present.	S. 1.	τιμῶ	τιμῶμαι	ποιῶ	ποιοῦμαι	δηλῶ	δηλοῦμαι
	2.	τιμᾷς	τιμᾷ	ποιεῖς	ποιῇ, ποιεῖ	δηλοῖς	δηλοῖ
	3.	τιμᾷ	τιμᾶται	ποιεῖ	ποιεῖται	δηλοῖ	δηλοῦται
	D. 2.	τιμᾶτον	τιμᾶσθον	ποιεῖτον	ποιεῖσθον	δηλοῦτον	δηλοῦσθον
	3.	τιμᾶτον	τιμᾶσθον	ποιεῖτον	ποιεῖσθον	δηλοῦτον	δηλοῦσθον
	P. 1.	τιμῶμεν	τιμώμεθα	ποιοῦμεν	ποιούμεθα	δηλοῦμεν	δηλούμεθα
	2.	τιμᾶτε	τιμᾶσθε	ποιεῖτε	ποιεῖσθε	δηλοῦτε	δηλοῦσθε
	3.	τιμῶσι(ν)	τιμῶνται	ποιοῦσι(ν)	ποιοῦνται	δηλοῦσι(ν)	δηλοῦνται
Imperfect.	S. 1.	ἐτίμων	ἐτιμώμην	ἐποίουν	ἐποιούμην	ἐδήλουν	ἐδηλούμην
	2.	ἐτίμᾱς	ἐτιμῶ	ἐποίεις	ἐποιοῦ	ἐδήλους	ἐδηλοῦ
	3.	ἐτίμᾱ	ἐτιμᾶτο	ἐποίει	ἐποιεῖτο	ἐδήλου	ἐδηλοῦτο
	D. 2.	ἐτιμᾶτον	ἐτιμᾶσθον	ἐποιεῖτον	ἐποιεῖσθον	ἐδηλοῦτον	ἐδηλοῦσθον
	3.	ἐτιμάτην	ἐτιμάσθην	ἐποιείτην	ἐποιείσθην	ἐδηλούτην	ἐδηλούσθην
	P. 1.	ἐτιμῶμεν	ἐτιμώμεθα	ἐποιοῦμεν	ἐποιούμεθα	ἐδηλοῦμεν	ἐδηλούμεθα
	2.	ἐτιμᾶτε	ἐτιμᾶσθε	ἐποιεῖτε	ἐποιεῖσθε	ἐδηλοῦτε	ἐδηλοῦσθε
	3.	ἐτίμων	ἐτιμῶντο	ἐποίουν	ἐποιοῦντο	ἐδήλουν	ἐδηλοῦντο

	ACTIVE.	PASS. AND MID.	ACT.	PASS. AND MID.	ACT.	PASS. AND MID.
S. 1.	τιμῶ	τιμῶμαι	ποιῶ	ποιῶμαι	δηλῶ	δηλῶμαι
2.	τιμᾷς	τιμᾷ	ποιῇς	ποιῇ	δηλοῖς	δηλοῖ
3.	τιμᾷ	τιμᾶται	ποιῇ	ποιῆται	δηλοῖ	δηλῶται
D. 2.	τιμᾶτον	τιμᾶσθον	ποιῆτον	ποιῆσθον	δηλῶτον	δηλῶσθον
3.	τιμᾶτον	τιμᾶσθον	ποιῆτον	ποιῆσθον	δηλῶτον	δηλῶσθον
P. 1.	τιμῶμεν	τιμώμεθα	ποιῶμεν	ποιώμεθα	δηλῶμεν	δηλώμεθα
2.	τιμᾶτε	τιμᾶσθε	ποιῆτε	ποιῆσθε	δηλῶτε	δηλῶσθε
3.	τιμῶσι(ν)	τιμῶνται	ποιῶσι(ν)	ποιῶνται	δηλῶσι(ν)	δηλῶνται
Optative.						
S. 1.	τιμ(ῷμι), ῴην	τιμῴμην	ποι(οῖμι), οίην	ποιοίμην	δηλ(οῖμι), οίην	δηλοίμην
2.	τιμ(ῷς), ῴης	τιμῷο	ποι(οῖς), οίης	ποιοῖο	δηλ(οῖς), οίης	δηλοῖο
3.	τιμ(ῷ), ῴη	τιμῷτο	ποιοῖ, οίη	ποιοῖτο	δηλοῖ, οίη	δηλοῖτο
D. 2.	τιμῷτον, (ῴητον)	τιμῷσθον	ποιοῖτον, (οίητον)	ποιοῖσθον	δηλοῖτον, (οίητον)	δηλοῖσθον
3.	τιμῴτην, (ῳήτην)	τιμῴσθην	ποιοίτην, (οιήτην)	ποιοίσθην	δηλοίτην, (οιήτην)	δηλοίσθην
P. 1.	τιμῷμεν, (ῴημεν)	τιμῴμεθα	ποιοῖμεν, (οίημεν)	ποιοίμεθα	δηλοῖμεν, (οίημεν)	δηλοίμεθα
2.	τιμῷτε, (ῴητε)	τιμῷσθε	ποιοῖτε, (οίητε)	ποιοῖσθε	δηλοῖτε, (οίητε)	δηλοῖσθε
3.	τιμῷεν, (ῴησαν)	τιμῷντο	ποιοῖεν, (οίησαν)	ποιοῖντο	δηλοῖεν, (οίησαν)	δηλοῖντο

		ACTIVE.	PASS. AND MID.	ACTIVE.	PASS. AND MID.	ACTIVE.	PASS. AND MID.
Imperative.	S. 2.	τίμα	τιμῶ	ποίει	ποιοῦ	δήλου	δηλοῦ
	3.	τιμάτω	τιμάσθω	ποιείτω	ποιείσθω	δηλούτω	δηλούσθω
	D. 2.	τιμᾶτον	τιμᾶσθον	ποιεῖτον	ποιεῖσθον	δηλοῦτον	δηλοῦσθον
	3.	τιμάτων	τιμάσθων	ποιείτων	ποιείσθων	δηλούτων	δηλούσθων
	P. 2.	τιμᾶτε	τιμᾶσθε	ποιεῖτε	ποιεῖσθε	δηλοῦτε	δηλοῦσθε
	3.	τιμάτωσαν or τιμώντων	τιμάσθωσαν or τιμάσθων	ποιείτωσαν or ποιούντων	ποιείσθωσαν or ποιείσθων	δηλούτωσαν or δηλούντων	δηλούσθωσαν or δηλούσθων
Inf.		τιμᾶν	τιμᾶσθαι	ποιεῖν	ποιεῖσθαι	δηλοῦν	δηλοῦσθαι
Partc.		τιμῶν, ῶσα, τιμῶν	τιμώμενος, η, ον	ποιῶν, ποιοῦσα, ποιοῦν	ποιούμενος, η, ον	δηλῶν, δηλοῦσα, δηλοῦν	δηλούμενος, η, ον

Fut. τιμήσω, τιμήσομαι. ποιήσω, ποιήσομαι δηλώσω, δηλώσομαι.

Perf. τετίμηκα, τετίμημαι. πεποίηκα, πεποίημαι. δεδήλωκα, δεδήλωμαι.

VERBS IN Ω.

CONSONANT-STEMS. I. In Gutturals.

πλέκω, *I plait*; φεύγω, *I flee*; τάσσω, *I arrange*. VERBAL-STEMS πλεκ, φυγ, ταχ.

ACTIVE VOICE.

PRESENT.	FUTURE.	AORIST.	PERFECT.
πλέκ-ω φεύγ-ω τάσσ-ω (for ταχιω)	πλέξ-ω φεύξ-ομαι τάξ-ω	ἔ-πλεξ-α (weak) ἔ-φυγ-ον (strong) ἔ-ταξ-α (weak)	πέ-πλεχ-α (weak) πέ-φευγ-α (strong) τέ-ταχ-α (weak)

MIDDLE AND PASSIVE VOICES.

PRESENT.	FUTURE.	AOR. MID. WEAK.	PERFECT.	FUTURE PERF.	AORIST PASSIVE.	FUT. PASSIVE.
πλέκ-ομαι τάσσ-ομαι	πλέξ-ομαι τάξ-ομαι	ἐ-πλεξ-άμην ἐ-ταξ-άμην	πέ-πλεγ-μαι τέ-ταγ-μαι	πε-πλέξ-ομαι τε-τάξ-ομαι	ἐπλάκ-ην (strong) ἐτάχ-θην (weak)	πλακήσ-ομαι ταχθήσ-ομαι

CONSONANT-STEMS. II. In Dentals.

ψεύδομαι, *I lie*; πείθω, *I persuade*; κομίζω, *I carry*. VERBAL-STEMS ψευδ, πιθ, κομιδ.

ACTIVE VOICE.

PRESENT.	FUTURE.	AORIST.	PERFECT.
πείθ-ω κομίζ-ω	πείσ-ω κομιῶ	ἔ-πεισ-α (weak) ἐ-κόμισ-α	πέ-ποιθ-α (strong) κε-κόμικ-α (weak)

MIDDLE AND PASSIVE VOICES.

PRESENT.	FUTURE.	AOR. MID. WEAK.	PERFECT.	AOR. PASS. WEAK.	FUT. PASS. WEAK.
ψεύδ-ομαι πείθ-ομαι κομίζ-ομαι	ψεύσ-ομαι πείσ-ομαι κομιοῦμαι	ἐ-ψευσ-άμην ἐ-πεισ-άμην ἐ-κομισ-άμην	ἔ-ψευσ-μαι πέ-πεισ-μαι κε-κόμισ-μαι	ἐ-ψεύσ-θην ἐ-πείσ-θην ἐ-κομίσ-θην	ψευσθήσ-ομαι πεισθήσ-ομαι κομισθήσ-ομαι

CONSONANT-STEMS. III. In Labials.

πέμπω, I send; λείπω, I leave; καλύπτω, I cover. VERBAL-STEMS πεμπ, λιπ, καλυβ.

ACTIVE VOICE.

PRESENT.	FUTURE.	AORIST.	PERFECT.
πέμπ-ω λείπ-ω καλύπτ-ω	πέμψ-ω λείψ-ω καλύψ-ω	ἔ-πεμψ-α (weak) ἔ-λιπ-ον (strong) ἐ-κάλυψ-α (weak)	πέ-πομφ-α (strong) λέ-λοιπ-α (strong)

MIDDLE AND PASSIVE VOICES.

PRESENT.	FUTURE.	AORIST MIDDLE.	PERFECT.	FUTURE PERF.	AOR. PASS. WEAK.	FUTURE PASS. WEAK.
πέμπ-ομαι λείπ-ομαι καλύπτ-ομαι	πέμψ-ομαι λείψ-ομαι καλύψ-ομαι	ἐ-πεμψ-άμην ἐ-λιπ-όμην (strong) ἐ-καλυψ-άμην	πέ-πεμ-μαι λέ-λειμ-μαι κε-κάλυμ-μαι	λε-λείψ-ομαι κε-καλύψ-ομαι	ἐ-πέμφ-θην ἐ-λείφ-θην ἐ-καλύφ-θην	πεμφθήσ-ομαι λειφθήσ-ομαι καλυφθήσ-ομαι

Consonant-Stems. IV. In Liquids.

δέρω, *I skin*; ἀγγέλλω, *I announce*; σπείρω, *I sow*. Verbal-Stems δερ, ἀγγελ, σπερ.

Active Voice.

PRESENT.	FUTURE.	AORIST.	PERFECT.
δέρ-ω ἀγγέλλ-ω (for ἀγγελ-ι-ω) σπείρ-ω (for σπερ-ι-ω)	δερῶ ἀγγελῶ σπερῶ	ἔ-δειρ-α ἤγγειλ-α ἔ-σπειρ-α } weak	ἤγγελκ-α ἔσπαρκ-α } weak

Middle and Passive Voices.

PRESENT.	FUTURE.	AOR. MID. WEAK.	PERFECT.	AORIST PASSIVE.	FUTURE PASSIVE.
δέρ-ομαι ἀγγέλλ-ομαι σπείρ-ομαι	δεροῦμαι ἀγγελοῦμαι σπεροῦμαι	ἐ-δειρ-άμην ἠγγειλ-άμην ἐ-σπειρ-άμην	δέ-δαρ-μαι ἤγγελ-μαι ἔ-σπαρ-μαι	ἐ-δάρ-ην (strong) ἠγγέλ-θην (weak) ἐ-σπάρ-ην	δαρήσ-ομαι (strong) ἀγγελθήσ-ομαι (weak) σπαρήσ-ομαι (strong)

REMARKS ON THE CONSONANT-STEMS.

1. The Consonant is changed before the person-ending according to the following rules:—

GUTTURAL AND LABIAL STEMS.

Hard letters must precede Hard.
Soft " " Soft.
Aspirate " " Aspirate.

Before μ Labials become μ, Gutturals γ.

DENTAL STEMS.

Dentals are dropped before σ or κ. Before any other consonant they become σ.

LIQUID AND NASAL STEMS.

λ and ρ remain unchanged.
ν is usually dropped before σ, θ, μ, τ, κ.

2. Between two Consonants σ is dropped.

3. All Verbs in Consonant-Stems form the 3rd Pers. Pl. Perf. Mid. with the Perf. Partc. and εἰσί(ν).

4. In Liquid and Nasal Verbs the Future Active is formed by adding -εσω, -εσομαι to the Verb-stem. The σ always drops out and the vowels are contracted, as in γένους for γενεσ-ος, *e.g.*—

Verb-stem, } Fut. Act. σπερ-ε-σω, σπερ-ε-ω, σπερῶ.
σπερ, *sow.* } Fut. Mid. σπερ-ε-σομαι, σπερ-ε-ομαι, σπεροῦμαι.

5. In Liquid and Nasal Verbs σ is dropped from -σα, -σάμην, the terminations of the Weak Aor. Act. and Mid. and the vowel of the stem is lengthened in compensation, *e.g.*—

Verb-stem, } Aor. Act. ἐσπερ-σα, ἔσπειρα.
σπερ, *sow* } Aor. Mid. ἐσπερ-σαμην, ἐσπειράμην.

VERBS IN -μι.

-θε. FIRST CLASS.—Verbs which affix their endings directly to the stem. The Present stem is often the Verb-stem reduplicated. τί-θη-μι, *I place.* Verb-stem θε.

ACTIVE VOICE.

TENSES.		INDICATIVE.		SUBJUNC.	OPTATIVE.	IMPERATIVE.	INF.	PARTC.
		Present.	*Imperfect.*					
Present and Imperfect. Stem τιθε.	S. 1.	τί-θη-μι	ἐ-τί-θη-ν	τι-θῶ	τι-θείην	—	τι-θέ-ναι	τι-θεί-ς, τι-θεῖ-σα, τι-θέ-ν. st. τι-θε-ντ.
	2.	τί-θη-ς	ἐ-τί-θεις	τι-θῇ-ς	τι-θείης	τί-θει		
	3.	τί-θη-σι(ν)	ἐ-τί-θει	τι-θῇ	τι-θείη	τι-θέ-τω		
	D. 2.	τί-θε-τον	ἐ-τί-θε-τον	τι-θῆ-τον	τι-θείητον, τι-θεῖτον	τί-θε-τον		
	3.	τί-θε-τον	ἐ-τι-θέ-την	τι-θῆ-τον	τι-θειήτην, τι-θείτην	τι-θέ-των		
	P. 1.	τί-θε-μεν	ἐ-τί-θε-μεν	τι-θῶ-μεν	τι-θείημεν, τι-θεῖμεν	—		
	2.	τί-θε-τε	ἐ-τί-θε-τε	τι-θῆ-τε	τι-θείητε, τι-θεῖτε	τί-θε-τε		
	3.	τι-θέ-ᾱ-σι(ν)	ἐ-τί-θε-σαν	τι-θῶ-σι(ν)	τι-θείησαν, τι-θεῖεν	τι-θέ-τωσαν or τι-θέ-ντων		
Aorist. Stem θε.	S. 1.		ἔ-θη-κ-α (weak)	θῶ	θείην	—	θεῖ-ναι	θεί-ς, θεῖ-σα, θέ-ν. st. θε-ντ.
	2.		ἔ-θη-κ-ας (weak)	θῇ-ς	θείης	θέ-ς		
	3.		ἔ-θη-κ-ε(ν) (weak)	θῇ	θείη	θέ-τω		
	D. 2.		ἔ-θε-τον	θῆ-τον	θείητον, θεῖτον	θέ-τον		
	3.		ἐ-θέ-την	θῆ-τον	θειήτην, θείτην	θέ-των		
	P. 1.		ἔ-θε-μεν	θῶ-μεν	θείημεν, θεῖμεν	—		
	2.		ἔ-θε-τε	θῆ-τε	θείητε, θεῖτε	θέ-τε		
	3.		ἔ-θε-σαν or ἔ-θη-κ-αν	θῶ-σι(ν)	θείησαν, θεῖεν	θέ-τωσαν or θέ-ντων		

MIDDLE AND PASSIVE VOICE.

TENSES.		INDICATIVE.		SUBJUNCTIVE.	OPTATIVE.	IMPERATIVE.	INF.	PARTC.
		Present.	*Imperfect.*					
Present and Imperfect. Stem τιθε.	S. 1.	τί-θε-μαι	ἐ-τι-θέ-μην	τι-θῶ-μαι	τι-θεί-μην	—	τί-θε-σθαι	τι-θέ-μενος, η, ον.
	2.	τί-θε-σαι	ἐ-τί-θε-σο	τι-θῇ	τι-θεῖ-ο	τί-θε-σο		
	3.	τί-θε-ται	ἐ-τί-θε-το	τι-θῆ-ται	τι-θεῖ-το	τι-θέ-σθω		
	D. 2.	τί-θε-σθον	ἐ-τί-θε-σθον	τι-θῆ-σθον	τι-θεῖ-σθον	τί-θε-σθον		
	3.	τί-θε-σθον	ἐ-τι-θέ-σθην	τι-θῆ-σθον	τι-θεί-σθην	τι-θέ-σθων		
	P. 1.	τι-θέ-μεθα	ἐ-τι-θέ-μεθα	τι-θώ-μεθα	τι-θεί-μεθα	—		
	2.	τί-θε-σθε	ἐ-τί-θε-σθε	τι-θῆ-σθε	τι-θεῖ-σθε	τί-θε-σθε		
	3.	τί-θε-νται	ἐ-τί-θε-ντο	τι-θῶ-νται	τι-θεῖ-ντο	τι-θέ-σθωσαν or τι-θέ-σθων		
Strong Aorist. Stem θε.			ἐ-θέ-μην	θῶ-μαι	θεί-μην	—	θέ-σθαι	θέ-μενος, η, ον.
			ἔ-θου	θῇ	θεῖ-ο	θοῦ		
			ἔ-θε-το	θῆ-ται	θεῖ-το	θέ-σθω		
			&c. as Imperft.	&c. as Present.	&c. as Present.	&c. as Present.		

Aorist Pass., ἐτέθην. *Weak Future Pass.*, τεθήσομαι. [*Perfect Mid.*, τέθειμαι.]

Obs. ἵη-μι, *I send* (Verb-stem ἑ), is inflected throughout like τί-θη-μι.

VERBS IN -μι.

FIRST CLASS.—ἵ-στη-μι, *I make to stand.* Verb-stem στα.—ACTIVE VOICE.

TENSE.		INDICATIVE. Present.	INDICATIVE. Imperfect.	SUBJUNCTIVE.	OPTATIVE.	IMPERATIVE.	INF.	PARTC.
Present and Imperf. Stem, ἱστα.	S. 1.	ἵ-στη-μι	ἵ-στη-ν	ἱ-στῶ	ἱ-σταίην	—	ἱ-στά-ναι	ἱ-στά-ς, ἱ-στᾶ-σα, ἱ-στάν. Stem, ἱ-σταντ.
	2.	ἵ-στη-ς	ἵ-στη-ς	ἱ-στῇ-ς	ἱ-σταίης	ἵ-στη		
	3.	ἵ-στη-σι(ν)	ἵ-στη	ἱ-στῇ	ἱ-σταίη	ἱ-στά-τω		
	D. 2.	ἵ-στα-τον	ἵ-στα-τον	ἱ-στῆ τον	ἱ-σταίητον, ἱ-σταῖτον	ἵ-στα-τον		
	3.	ἵ-στα-τον	ἱ-στά-την	ἱ-στῆ-τον	ἱ-σταιήτην, ἱ-σταίτην	ἱ-στά-των		
	P. 1.	ἵ-στα-μεν	ἵ-στα-μεν	ἱ-στῶ-μεν	ἱ-σταίημεν, ἱ-σταῖμεν	—		
	2.	ἵ-στα-τε	ἵ-στα-τε	ἱ-στῆ-τε	ἱ-σταίητε, ἱ-σταῖτε	ἵ-στα-τε		
	3.	ἱ-στᾶ-σι(ν)	ἵ-στα-σαν	ἱ-στῶ-σι(ν)	ἱ-σταίησαν, ἱ-σταῖεν	ἱ-στά-τωσαν or ἱ-στά-ντων		
Strong Aorist. Stem, στα.	S. 1.		ἔ-στη-ν	στῶ	σταίην	—	στῆ-ναι	στά-ς, στᾶ-σα, στάν. Stem, σταντ.
	2.		ἔ-στη-ς	στῇ-ς	σταίης	στῆ-θι		
	3.		ἔ-στη	στῇ	σταίη	στή-τω		
	D. 2.		ἔ-στη-τον	στῆ-τον	σταίητον, σταῖτον	στῆ-τον		
	3.		ἐ-στή-την	στῆ-τον	σταιήτην, σταίτην	στή-των		
	P. 1.		ἔ-στη-μεν	στῶ-μεν	σταίημεν, σταῖμεν	—		
	2.		ἔ-στη-τε	στῆ-τε	σταίητε, σταῖτε	στῆ-τε		
	3.		ἔ-στη-σαν	στῶ-σι(ν)	σταίησαν, σταῖεν	στή-τωσαν or στά-ντων		

Fut. στήσω. *Weak Aor.* ἔστησα. *Perf.* ἕστηκα.

In the Pres., Fut., and weak Aor. the meaning is transitive, *make to stand;* but in strong Aor. and Perf. intransitive *I stood* and *I stand*.

Middle and Passive Voices.

Tenses.		Indicative. Present.	Indicative. Imperfect.	Subjunctive.	Optative.	Imperative.	Inf.	Partc.
Present and Imperfect. Stem ἱστα.	S. 1.	ἵ-στα-μαι	ἱ-στά-μην	ἱ-στῶ-μαι	ἱ-σταί-μην	—	ἵ-στα-σθαι	ἱ-στά-μενος, η, ον.
	2.	ἵ-στα-σαι	ἵ-στα-σο	ἱ-στῇ	ἱ-σταῖ-ο	ἵ-στα-σο		
	3.	ἵ-στα-ται	ἵ-στα-το	ἱ-στῆ-ται	ἱ-σταῖ-το	ἱ-στά-σθω		
	D. 2.	ἵ-στα-σθον	ἵ-στα-σθον	ἱ-στῆ-σθον	ἱ-σταῖ-σθον	ἵ-στα-σθον		
	3.	ἵ-στα-σθον	ἱ-στά-σθην	ἱ-στῆ-σθον	ἱ-σταί-σθην	ἱ-στά-σθων		
	P. 1.	ἱ-στά-μεθα	ἱ-στά-μεθα	ἱ-στώ-μεθα	ἱ-σταί-μεθα	—		
	2.	ἵ-στα-σθε	ἵ-στα-σθε	ἱ-στῆ-σθε	ἱ-σταῖ-σθε	ἵ-στα-σθε		
	3.	ἵ-στα-νται	ἵ-στα-ντο	ἱ-στῶ-νται	ἱ-σταῖ-ντο	ἱ-στά-σθωσαν or ἱ-στά-σθων		
Strong Aorist.		Wanting.						

Fut., στήσομαι. *Weak Aorist Pass.*, ἐστάθην. *Weak Fut. Pass.*, σταθήσομαι.

ἐστησάμην, the Weak Aor. Mid., is always transitive.

VERBS IN -μι.

FIRST CLASS.—δί-δω-μι, *I offer*. Verb-stem δο.

ACTIVE VOICE.

TENSES.		INDICATIVE.		SUBJUNCTIVE.	OPTATIVE.	IMPERATIVE.	INF.	PARTC.
		Present.	*Imperfect.*					
Present and Imperfect. Stem δ.δο.	S. 1.	δί-δω-μι	ἐ-δί-δουν	δι-δῶ	δι-δοίην	—	δι-δό-ναι	δι-δού-ς, δι-δοῦ-σα, δι-δό-ν. stem δι-δο-ντ.
	2.	δί-δω-ς	ἐ-δί-δους	δι-δῷ-ς	δι-δοίης	δί-δου		
	3.	δί-δω-σι(ν)	ἐ-δί-δου	δι-δῷ	δι-δοίη	δι-δό-τω		
	D. 2.	δί-δο-τον	ἐ-δί-δο-τον	δι-δῶ-τον	δι-δοίητον, διδοῖτον	δί-δο-τον		
	3.	δί-δο-τον	ἐ-δι-δό-την	δι-δῶ-τον	δι-δοιήτην, διδοίτην	δι-δό-των		
	P. 1.	δί-δο-μεν	ἐ-δί-δο-μεν	δι-δῶ-μεν	δι-δοίημεν, διδοῖμεν	—		
	2.	δί-δο-τε	ἐ-δί-δο-τε	δι-δῶ-τε	δι-δοίητε, διδοῖτε	δί-δο-τε		
	3.	δι-δό-ᾱσι(ν)	ἐ-δί-δο-σαν	δι-δῶ-σι(ν)	δι-δοίησαν, διδοῖεν	δι-δό-τωσαν or δι-δό-ντων		
		Weak.	*Strong.*					
Aorist. Stem δο.	S. 1.	ἔ-δω-κ-α	—	δῶ	δοίην	—	δοῦ-ναι	δού-ς, δοῦ-σα, δό-ν. stem δο-ντ.
	2.	ἔ-δω-κ-ας	—	δῷ-ς	δοίης	δό-ς		
	3.	ἔ-δω-κ-ε	—	δῷ	δοίη	δό-τω		
	D. 2.	—	ἔ-δο-τον	δῶ-τον	δοίητον, δοῖτον	δό-τον		
	3.	—	ἐ-δό-την	δῶ-τον	δοιήτην, δοίτην	δό-των		
	P. 1.	ἐ-δώ-κ-αμεν	ἔ-δο-μεν	δῶ-μεν	δοίημεν, δοῖμεν	—		
	2.	ἐ-δώ-κ-ατε	ἔ-δο-τε	δῶ-τε	δοίητε, δοῖτε	δό-τε		
	3.	ἔ-δω-κ-αν	ἔ-δο-σαν	δῶ-σι(ν)	δοίησαν, δοῖεν	δό-τωσαν or δό-ντων		

Fut., δώσω. *Perf.*, δέδωκα.

MIDDLE VOICE.

TENSES.		INDICATIVE. Present.	Imperfect.	SUBJUNCTIVE.	OPTATIVE.	IMPERATIVE.	INF.	PARTC.
Present and Imperfect. Stem διδο.	S. 1	δί-δο-μαι	ἐ-δι-δό-μην	δι-δῶ-μαι	δι-δοί-μην	—	δί-δο-σθαι	δι-δό-μενος, η, ον.
	2.	δί-δο-σαι	ἐ-δί-δο-σο	δι-δῷ	δι-δοῖ-ο	δί-δο-σο		
	3.	δί-δο-ται	ἐ-δί-δο-το	δι-δῶ-ται	δι-δοῖ-το	δι-δό-σθω		
	D. 2.	δί-δο-σθον	ἐ-δί-δο-σθον	δι-δῶ-σθον	δι-δοῖ-σθον	δί-δο-σθον		
	3.	δί-δο-σθον	ἐ-δι-δό-σθην	δι-δῶ-σθον	δι-δοί-σθην	δι-δό-σθων		
	P. 1.	δι-δό-μεθα	ἐ-δι-δό-μεθα	δι-δώ-μεθα	δι-δοί-μεθα	—		
	2.	δί-δο-σθε	ἐ-δί-δο-σθε	δι-δῶ-σθε	δι-δοῖ-σθε	δί-δο-σθε		
	3.	δί-δο-νται	ἐ-δί-δο-ντο	δι-δῶ-νται	δι-δοῖ-ντο	δι-δόσθωσαν or διδό-σθων		
Strong Aorist. Stem δο.			ἐ-δό-μην	δῶ-μαι	δοί-μην	—	δό-σθαι	δό-μενος, η, ον.
			ἔ-δου	δῷ	δοῖ-ο	δοῦ		
			ἔ-δο-το	δῶ-ται	δοῖ-το	δό-σθω		
			&c. as Imperf.	&c. as Present.	&c. as Present.	&c. as Present.		

Perf., δέδομαι. *Weak Aor. Pass.*, ἐδόθην. *Weak Fut. Pass.*, δοθήσομαι.

VERBS IN -μι.

The forms of the verb εἶμι, *I shall go* (Verb-stem ι) are as follows :—

	Indicative: *Present.*	Indicative: *Imperfect.*		Subjunctive.	Optative.	Imperative.	Inf.	Partc.
S. 1.	εἶ-μι	ᾔειν or ᾔα		ἴω	ἴοιμι or ἰοίην	—	ἰέναι.	ἰών, ἰοῦσα, ἰόν. Stem ἰοντ.
2.	εἶ	ᾔεις	ᾔεισθα	ἴῃς	ἴοις	ἴθι		
3.	εἶ-σι(ν)	ᾔει	ᾔειν	ἴῃ	ἴοι	ἴτω		
D. 2.	ἴ-τον	ᾔειτον	ᾖτον	ἴητον	ἴοιτον	ἴτον		
3.	ἴ-τον	ᾐείτην	ᾔτην	ἴητον	ἰοίτην	ἴτων		
P. 1.	ἴ-μεν	ᾔειμεν	ᾖμεν	ἴωμεν	ἴοιμεν	—		
2.	ἴ-τε	ᾔειτε	ᾖτε	ἴητε	ἴοιτε	ἴτε		
3.	ἴ-ᾱσι(ν)	ᾔεσαν		ἴωσι(ν)	ἴοιεν	ἴτωσαν or ἰόντων		

VERBS IN -μι.

Second Class.—Verbs which form the Present-Stem by adding νυ to the Pure Stem.

δείκ-νυ-μι, *I shew*. Pure Stem, δεικ. Present-Stem, δεικ-νυ.

	Present Indic. Active.	*Present Indic. Mid. and Pass.*
Sing.	δείκ-νῡ-μι	δείκ-νῠ-μαι
	δείκ-νῡ-ς	δείκ-νῠ-σαι
	δείκ-νῡ-σι(ν)	δείκ-νῠ-ται
Dual.	δείκ-νῠ-τον	δείκ-νυ-σθον
	δείκ-νῠ-τον	δείκ-νυ-σθον
Plur.	δείκ-νῠ-μεν	δεικ-νύ-μεθα
	δείκ-νῠ-τε	δείκ-νυ-σθε
	δεικ-νύ-ᾱσι(ν)	δείκ-νυ-νται
	Imperfect	*Imperfect.*
	ἐ-δείκ-νῡ-ν, &c.	ἐ-δεικ-νύ-μην, &c.
	Imperative.	*Imperative.*
	δείκ-νῡ, &c.	δείκ-νῠ-σο, &c.

Inf. Act. δεικ-νύ-ναι. Mid. δείκ-νυ-σθαι. The other tenses and moods are like those of verbs in -ω. Subj. δεικ-νύ-ω, &c.; and even in the Pres. and Imperf. Ind. and the Imperative forms like δεικ-νύ-εις for δείκ-νῡ-ς are very common.

PART II.

CHAPTER I.

On §§ I.—V.

1. The forms which you have learned in the preceding Part of this Book belong to the Attic Dialect of the Greek Language. Other dialects were the Doric, the Ionic, and the Aeolic. The poems of Homer were written in the Ionic dialect, and in the history of Herodotus we see a later form of the same. The Attic is really an offshoot of the Ionic, as the Athenians who inhabited Attica belonged to the Ionian race. But Attic writers struck out a path for themselves, and by the number and excellence of their writings, gave so great importance to the refined Ionic in which they wrote that the Attic must be regarded as distinct from the Ionic. The chief writers in the Attic dialect were the orators Andocides, Antiphon, Lysias, Isocrates, Isæus, Aeschines, and Demosthenes, the historians Thucydides and Xenophon, the philosopher Plato, and the Comic poet Aristophanes. The Tragic poets Aeschylus, Sophocles, and Euripides, wrote in Attic, but many forms were allowed in Tragedy which could not be used in pure Attic.

2. A very small portion of Attic literature has come down to us, but it is surprising that so much should have been

preserved. For the difficulty of multiplying the copies of an ancient book was very great. All books had to be copied by scribes, and the only letters known were the large and clumsy capitals which could not be written quickly. The small or cursive letters in which Greek books are printed did not come into general use among manuscript copyists till the eighth century after Christ, or about twelve hundred years after the great Attic authors named above wrote.

3. **The Alphabet.**—You will observe that, although there are twenty-four letters, there are not twenty-four distinct sounds in the Greek alphabet. There is no essential difference of sound between ε and η, ο and ω. In fact η and ω did not exist in the early Greek alphabet, but E and O served to represent both the long and the short sound of the two letters. The other three vowels have each only one letter-sign, which is used indifferently for their long and their short sound. Moreover ξ is simply κσ and ψ is πσ, and the sound of ζ might probably have been given by δσ, while σσ, which is as much a double letter as ξ, ψ, or ζ, has no separate character. On the other hand γ has two distinct sounds—a guttural and a nasal. When used as a nasal [ἄγγελος, ἀγκύρα, Ἀγχίσης] it is sometimes called ἄγμα.

One letter which was in use when Homer wrote the *Iliad* and *Odyssey* afterwards disappeared from the Greek alphabet. Its name and shape are uncertain, but it was pronounced like our *F* or *V*. Both the name Digamma, by which it is now known, and the form Ϝ are late inventions.

The distinction now made between σ and ς was not known till books began to be printed in Greek. The form ς is of course only the ordinary σ with the last turn directed downwards instead of upwards. When the first part of a compound word ends in sigma, ς is sometimes used, as προςάγω [πρὸς, ἄγω]. The form ϑ, which is often used for theta, is only a shorter way of writing θ.

4. **Vowels.**—Attic Greek had twenty-two Vowel sounds, namely, ᾰ, ᾱ; ε, η; ῐ, ῑ; ο, ω; ῠ, ῡ; αι, ει, οι; αυ, ευ, ου; ᾱͅ, ῃ, ῳ; ᾱυ, ηυ; υι. The Diphthongs were produced by the union of the hard vowels α, ε, η, ο, ω with the soft vowels ι and υ. When the hard vowel is long the diphthong is called improper, and if the soft vowel is ι it is written underneath the hard (iota subscript), as, ᾱͅ, ῃ, ῳ. When written in capitals, ᾳ, ῃ, ῳ appear as AI, HI, ΩI; or if a word beginning with such a diphthong requires a capital, the iota is still brought into line, as ῞Αιδης for ᾅδης. By the union of the two soft vowels the diphthong υι is produced.

5. **Consonants.**—The letters called gutturals ought rather to be called palatals, as the soft palate and not the throat is the organ in which the sound is formed. The dentals are also called linguals, which is a wider term, and includes not only the mutes, but also σ, λ, ν, and ρ. The letter μ, though not belonging to the mutes, is a labial. We may now arrange all the consonants in three classes.

Labials	π	β	φ	μ			
Gutturals	κ	γ	χ				
Linguals	τ	δ	θ	σ	λ	ν	ρ.

6. **Signs.**—Besides its use to mark the absence of the spiritus asper, the sign ' is also used to indicate the elision of one vowel before another, as ταῦτ' ἔφη for ταῦτα ἔφη, and to show that two words have been run together, as κᾆτα for καὶ εἶτα. In the first case it is called apostrophe, in the second coronis.

In writing Greek we use the same marks as in English for diaeresis, the full stop and the comma; but in Greek there is no note of exclamation, and the colon or semicolon is represented by · as ὥρα· while the English semicolon supplies the place of our note of interrogation, as τί ταῦτα; *what is this?* There are also three signs used to mark accent. In the sentence ἐγὼ ταῦτα λέγω, the accent of the first word is the grave, of the second the circumflex, and of the third the acute. Accents are written to the left of capitals, and on the second vowel of a diphthong, as Ὅμηρος, εὔστομος. It must be understood that all this last paragraph refers only to Greek as now written, and not at all to ancient Greek, which had no system of punctuation, and did not mark accents.

CHAPTER II.

On § VI.

7. The real difficulty of inflexion consists in the collision of the stem and the ending. Vowels collide with vowels, and consonants with consonants to form discordant sounds. Such discordancy is removed by the four methods of contraction, assimilation, dissimilation, and vowel compensation for consonantal loss. Contraction is used in the case of vowels; by the other three methods consonants are brought into harmony.

8. **Contraction.**—The Attic dialect used contraction wherever it was possible, and in a natural way. If you know the first part of this Grammar well, you will have no further difficulty with contraction. But you will have noticed a few inconsistencies, and some apparent difficulties. One

striking inconsistency is that in the Dual and Plural of the First Declension, and in Neuter nouns of the Second, εα contracts to α and not to η: as χρυσέᾰ, χρυσᾶ; χρυσέᾱς, χρυσᾶς; ὀστέᾰ, ὀστᾶ. In other cases, as in the Third Declension, this happens only when the εα is preceded by a vowel or ρ, as, ὑγιής, *healthy*, Acc. ὑγιᾶ. In εᾰς, of the Acc. Plural of the Third Declension, we find εᾰ contracted to ει, as, πήχεις for πήχεᾰς, πρέσβεις for πρέσβεᾰς.

In the Dual of the Third Declension εε sometimes becomes η, as ἄστη, εὐγενῆ. This happens also in the Nom. Plural of Masculine nouns in ευς, as βασιλῆς for βασιλέες. It is true that the broad sound of ο generally prevails over other sounds, but in Contracted Adjectives it disappears altogether before α, η, αι, ῃ; as διπλόα, διπλᾶ; διπλόη, διπλῆ; διπλόαι, διπλαῖ; διπλόῃ, διπλῇ.

9. **Assimilation.**—When two mutes come together, the latter of which is a dental, the former must be changed to the same order as the dental. Before a hard dental the other mute becomes hard, before a soft dental soft, and before an aspirate it becomes aspirated; or, referring to the table on page 2, the former letter must be changed so as to be in the same vertical column as the second. Thus:—

Before	τ	Gutturals	become	κ,	Labials	become	π.
,,	δ	,,	,,	γ,	,,	,,	β.
,,	θ	,,	,,	χ,	,,	,,	φ.

It is to Assimilation also that the following changes are due. Before μ, gutturals become γ, labials μ, and dentals σ. When ν comes before a labial it is changed into μ, before a guttural into γ, and before λ and ρ into λ and ρ.

Examples of these changes are—

μέμιγ-ται	to	μέμικ-ται	τέτριβ-ται	to	τέτριπ-ται
ἔχ-τέος	to	ἐκ-τέος	γέγραφ-ται	to	γέγραπ-ται
πλέκ-δην	to	πλέγ-δην	λείπ-δην	to	λείβ-δην
νύχ-δην	to	νύγ-δην	κρύφ-δην	to	κρύβ-δην
ἐπλέκ-θην	to	ἐπλέχ-θην	ἐπέμπ-θην	to	ἐπέμφ-θην
ἐζεύγ-θην	to	ἐζεύχ-θην	ἐτρίβ-θην	to	ἐτρίφ-θην

πέπλεκ-μαι	to	πέπλεγ-μαι
τέτυχ-μαι	to	τέτυγ-μαι
λέλειπ-μαι	to	λέλειμ-μαι
βλέβ-μα	to	βλέμ-μα
γραφ-μή	to	γραμ-μή
ἥνυτ-μαι	to	ἥνυσ-μαι
ἴδ-μεν	to	ἴσ-μεν
πέπειθ-μαι	to	πέπεισ-μαι
ἐν-πλέκω	to	ἐμ-πλέκω
ἐν-βάλλω	to	ἐμ-βάλλω
ἐν-φύω	to	ἐμ-φύω
ἐν-μίγνυμι	to	ἐμ-μίγνυμι
ἐν-κρατής	to	ἐγ-κρατής
ἐν-γράφω	to	ἐγ-γράφω
ἐν-χάσκω	to	ἐγ-χάσκω
ἐν-λείπω	to	ἐλ-λείπω
συν-ρέω	to	συρ-ρέω

10. **Dissimilation.**—By this is meant all such changes as θί-θημι into τί-θημι, and λύθη-θι into λύθη-τι. When a dental comes into collision with a dental, the first is changed to σ, as πέπειθται to πέπεισται. **Elision** may be regarded as Dissimilation extended. By Elision we understand the

simple disappearance of one of the discordant letters—as in λάμπας for λαμπαδς, and ἡγεμόσι for ἡγεμονσι.

Compensatory Lengthening.—You already know what is meant by this. In ὀδοῦσι the second syllable is long by nature, whereas in ὀδοντ-σι, which must have been its primitive form, the same syllable is long by position. In other words, to compensate for the loss of ντ, the vowel-sound was lengthened. In the case of α, ι, and υ the vowel simply becomes long instead of short, but ε like ο is lengthened to a diphthong.

CHAPTER III.

On § VII.

11. A STRIKING peculiarity in Greek is the Dual Number. Very few other languages possess it. In Latin there remain a few traces of it as in *duo*, *ambo*, *octo*. It is properly used only of things which go in pairs, as, *the ears*, *the eyes*, *the feet*, τὼ ὦτε, τὼ ὀφθαλμώ, τὼ πόδε, or of persons circumstanced alike, as, τὼ ἀδελφώ, *a pair of brothers*, τὼ ἵππω, *a span of horses*, τὼ πόλεε (πόλη), *two cities* in league with one another, or in some way circumstanced alike. Accordingly it is sometimes used with a Singular Verb. Even in cases like those mentioned above the place of the Dual may always be supplied by the Plural, but in the Attic dialect it occurs very frequently, and often with δύο or ἄμφω added. Thus we may use either τὼ τραπέζα or τὼ δύο τραπέζα, for *the two tables*. We may compare the way in which μικρόν is used with diminutives, as τὸ μικρὸν παιδάριον, *the little young child*.

12. But the Dual has not that completeness which the other two numbers have. Substantives have never more

than two distinct Dual forms—one representing the Nominative, Vocative, and Accusative Cases, and the other the Genitive and Dative. In fact in Attic two forms serve to express all the cases and genders Dual of the Article, of the Demonstrative and Relative Pronouns, and of all Adjectives in *ος, η, ον*, or *ος, ος, ον*, *e.g.*—

τώ	*τώ*	*τώ*
τοῖν	*τοῖν*	*τοῖν*
τούτω	*τούτω*	*τούτω*
τούτοιν	*τούτοιν*	*τούτοιν*
καλώ	*καλώ*	*καλώ*
καλοῖν	*καλοῖν*	*καλοῖν*

Moreover, Neuters in *ος* (st. *-εσ*) of the Third Declension have the same form for Nom., Voc., and Acc. Dual as for Nom., Voc., and Acc. Plural, *e.g.*, *τὼ γένη* and *τὰ γένη*. In words like *πόλις*, *πῆχυς*, and *ἄστυ*, the Dual is generally uncontracted, as, *πόλεε*, *ἄστεε*, *ἰχθυε*; but we sometimes find forms like *τὼ πόλη* or *τὼ πόλει*, *the two cities*, *τὼ πρέσβη*, *the two ambassadors*, *τὼ ἰχθῦ*, *the two fishes*.

13. The Active Voice of the Verb has no first person Dual, and the first person Dual of the Middle and Passive never occurs in Attic prose or Comedy.[1] In the principal tenses of the Indicative and in the Subjunctive there is only one form for the second and the third persons. The Imperative of the Middle Voice has no distinct form for the third person Dual, but uses the Plural form instead, *e.g.*, *λυσάσθων*, *let them loose for themselves*, or *let them two loose for themselves*.

[1] It occurs in classical Greek only thrice, Hom. *Il.* xxiii. 485, *περιδώμεθον*, Soph. *El.* 950, *λελείμμεθον*, and *Phil.* 1079, *ὁρμώμεθον*. We cannot accept as true Attic such forms as are found only in Tragedy, and the fact that in these three cases the metre would allow of the plural casts a doubt on the existence of words differing so little from the plural forms.

Further, even when Dual forms did exist, the Greeks often preferred to use a Plural Verb with a Substantive in the Dual.

14. Of the Cases you must pay special attention to the Vocative. The rules for forming the Vocative of the First Declension hold good in all cases, but Attic writers could also on emergency use the Nominative, as ὦ κριτὴς ἄριστε. In the Second Declension the true Vocative is much more frequent than the Nominative, except in the case of θεός, which has never its true Vocative form. In poetry, however, it is not unusual to find the Nominative used for the Vocative. In the Third Declension all is uncertain. It may be set down as a general rule that the Nominative may in all cases be used as a Vocative. Some words have no Vocative form distinct from the Nominative, and others, though possessed of a special form, rarely use it.

15. The following rules will help you to form the Vocative Case :—

(1) Stems which end in a Mute preceded by a Vowel have no Vocative form distinct from the Nominative, as, φυλακ, λαμπαδ, &c., Voc., φύλαξ, λάμπας.

Exceptions are Stems in -ιδ, as Ἄρτεμις (Stem Ἀρτεμιδ), Voc. Ἄρτεμι; τυραννίς (Stem τυραννιδ), Voc. τυραννί, *power;* παῖς (Stem παιδ, orig. παϊδ), Voc. παῖ, *boy.*

(2) Stems ending in ν or ρ preceded by a *long* Vowel have no Vocative distinct from the Nominative, as Ἕλλην, *Greek,* θήρ, *wild-beast.*

Exceptions are Ποσειδῶν, Voc. Πόσειδον (Stem Ποσειδων); Ἀπόλλων, Voc. Ἄπολλον (Stem Ἀπολλων); σωτήρ, *saviour,* Voc. σῶτερ (Stem σωτηρ); and sometimes Χάρων, *Charon,* Voc. Χάρον (Stem Χαρων).

(3) Stems ending in ν or ρ preceded by a short vowel *have no* separate Vocative form if the last syllable of the

Nominative is accented, as ἡγεμών, *leader*, Voc. ἡγεμών (Stem ἡγεμον); ἀήρ, *air*, Voc. ἀήρ (Stem ἀερ).

Exceptions are ἀηδών, *nightingale*, Voc. ἀηδοῖ (Stem ἀηδον); χελιδών, *swallow*, Voc. χελιδοῖ, or χελιδόν (Stem χελιδον); πατήρ, *father*, Voc. πάτερ (Stem πατερ).

(4) But if the last syllable is not accented, these Stems occasionally form a Vocative, as δαίμων, *deity*, Voc. δαῖμον (Stem δαιμον); μήτηρ, *mother*, Voc. μῆτερ (Stem μητερ); ῥήτωρ, *orator*, Voc. ῥῆτορ (Stem ῥητορ). Adjectives, κακοδαίμων, *unfortunate*, Voc. κακόδαιμον (Stem κακοδαιμον); τάλας, *wretched*, Voc. τάλᾰν (Stem ταλᾰν).

But in these cases the Nominative is still very often used as a Vocative. Thus we may have ὦ μήτηρ, ὦ κύων, ὦ ἀλάστωρ, ὦ κακοδαίμων, ὦ τάλας, ὦ μέλας, as well as ὦ μῆτερ, ὦ κύον, ὦ ἄλαστορ, ὦ κακόδαιμον, ὦ τάλαν, ὦ μέλαν.

(5) Stems ending in ντ have occasionally a Vocative, but by no means often. The Nominative form, except in a few words, is far the more common of the two. Thus Homer uses Αἶαν as the Vocative of Αἴας (Stem Αἰαντ), whereas Attic writers invariably prefer the Nominative form Αἴας. On the other hand γέρων, *old man* (Stem γεροντ), generally forms a Vocative γερον.

Adjectives are as uncertain as Substantives; thus χάριεν, *O graceful one* (Stem χαριεντ), is occasionally found; but ὦ χαρίεις is the more common.

Participles of the Third Declension have never a Vocative form.

(6) In Stems ending in diphthongs, the Vocative is generally distinct from the Nominative, being the pure Stem, as, ὦ βασιλεῦ, ὦ γραῦ, but even in this case the Nominative would not be wrong.

(7) In soft vowel-stems the Nominative is sometimes preferred, sometimes the true Vocative. Thus πόλι does occur,

but πόλις is far more common. So ὦ σύνεσις, or ὦ σύνεσι; ὦ ἰχθυ, or ὦ ἰχθυς, &c.

In the case of Adjectives, the Nominative is the more often found, as ὦ γλυκύς.

(8) Stems which elide sigma, as Δημοσθενες, generally form a Vocative, as ὦ Δημόσθενες (Nom. Δημοσθένης). In the case of Adjectives the Feminine and Masculine have the same form, as, ὦ δυστυχὲς ἄνερ, ὦ δυστυχὲς γύναι, *O unhappy man, O unhappy woman.* But the Nominative is also frequently used, as ὦ δυστυχὴς ἄνερ, ὦ δυστυχὴς γύναι.

(9) Stems in ο form the Vocative in οι, as αἰδώς (Stem αἰδο), *shame*, Voc. αἰδοῖ.

For Masculine Vocative, μέγας, *great*, generally used the Nominative, as ὦ μέγας αἰθήρ, but μέγα is found once or twice. μεγάλε, which occurs once in Aeschylus, is probably a licence.

In short there is no limit in Greek to the use of the Nominative for the Vocative. We may have ὦ ταλάντατος, ὦ Ἄρης, ὦ γυνή, ὦ κρίτης, or any other Nominative form.

CHAPTER IV.

On § VII. (3).

GENDER.

16. The Gender of Greek Substantives is ascertained sometimes by their meaning, sometimes by their form.

As in English, so in Greek, difference in sex may be expressed in different ways. In some cases distinct words are used, as, ὁ ἀνήρ, ἡ γυνή, *the man, the woman;* ὁ πατήρ, ἡ μήτηρ, *the father, the mother;* ὁ υἱός, ἡ θυγάτηρ, *the son, the daughter;* in others the distinction is made by means of termination, as, ὁ λέων, ἡ λέαινα, *the lion, the lioness;*

ὁ δεσπότης, ἡ δεσπότις, *the master, the mistress;* in others again the same form serves for both genders, as ὁ, ἡ θεός, *the god,* ὁ, ἡ μάρτυς, *the witness,* ὁ, ἡ παῖς, *the child.*

17. Of the names of beasts, most are common, as ὁ, ἡ κύων, ὁ, ἡ ἵππος, ὁ, ἡ βοῦς; but it occasionally happens that a word signifying an animal with sex has grammatically only one gender, as, ὁ δελφίς, *dolphin,* ὁ λαγώς, *hare,* ἡ ἀλώπηξ, *fox,* ἡ χελιδών, *swallow.* In such cases the gender when necessary was expressed by the words ἄρρην and θῆλυς, as ὁ θῆλυς λαγώς, *the she-hare,* ὁ θῆλυς δελφίς, *the she-dolphin,* ἡ ἄρρην χελιδών, *the male-swallow,* ἡ ἄρρην ἀλώπηξ, *the male-fox.*

18. Besides the names of Masculine beings, **Masculine** are the names of all winds and months, and of most rivers; as, ὁ Γαμηλιών, *the (month) Gamelion,* ὁ βορέας, *the north wind,* ὁ Ἰλισσος, *the (river) Ilissus.* The reason probably is that the Greek words for river, wind, and month—ποταμός, ἄνεμος, μήν—are all Masculine.

Exceptions.—Diminutives are Neuter, even when they signify males; as, τὸ ἀνθρώπιον, *the manikin.* τὸ ἀνδράποδον, *the slave,* is also Neuter.

A few names of rivers are Feminine. Of these the most notable are ἡ Λήθη, and ἡ Στύξ.

Most names of mountains are Masculine, but those ending in -ον are Neuter, and in -η Feminine. A few others are also Feminine, as, ἡ Πάρνης.

19. **Feminine** are the names of females, of lands, islands, cities, trees, and plants, and of abstract words, as, ἡ Ἀφροδίτη, *Aphrodite,* ἡ γυνή, *woman,* ἡ Λεόντιον, *Leontion,* ἡ Γλυκέριον, *Glycerium,* ἡ Ἀττική, *Attica,* ἡ Κέως, *the (island) Ceōs,* ἡ Λακεδαίμων, *the (city) Lacedaemon,* ἡ πίτυς, *the pine,* ἡ δικαιοσύνη, *justice.*

Exceptions.—Diminutives are Neuter even when they signify females, as τὸ γύναιον, *the little woman.* Of names *of countries,* Ἑλλήσποντος is Masculine, and Δέλτα Neuter.

Of the names of islands, those in -ον are Neuter.

Of the names of cities, there are many which are not Feminine. Of these the most common are τὸ Ἄργος, τὸ Ἴλιον, τὰ Ἄβδηρα, οἱ Δελφοί.

Of the names of trees and plants Masculine are φοῖνιξ, *palm*, φελλός, *cork*, κισσός, *ivy*, and some others; Neuter are those ending in -ον and -ι, as, πράσον, *leek*, πέπερι, *pepper*.

20. **Neuter** are the names of most fruits, of the letters, the Infinitive used substantivally, and every word when referred to merely as a word; as, τὸ μῆλον, *the apple*, τὸ σῖγμα, *sigma*, τὸ γυνή, *the* (word) *woman*, τὸ ζῆν, *life*.

21. **First Declension**, Masculine are all substantives which end in ας or ης; Feminine all in α, η.

22. **Second Declension**, Masculine are all substantives which end in ος, ως; Neuter those in ον, ων.

Exceptions.—All words in ον, ων are Neuter, except the names of women, as ἡ Γλυκέριον; but there are many words in ος which are Feminine. The most important you have learned on page 7. Others are:—

κέρκος, *tail.*
μήρινθος, *cord.*

τρίβος, *footpath.* ἁμαξιτός, *carriage road.* κάπετος, *ditch.*	Like κέλευθος, ἀτραπός, ὁδός, τάφρος.
κιβωτός, *chest.* χηλός, *coffer.* κάρδοπος, *kneading-trough.* πύελος, *bathing-tub.* λήκυθος, *oil-flask.* πρόχους (οος), *ewer.* ἄκατος, *boat.*	Things *hollow*, like ληνός, σορός, γνάθος, κάμινος.

σμάραγδος, *emerald.* σάπφειρος, *lapis lazuli.* μίλτος, *ochre.* ἄσφαλτος, *bitumen.* ἤλεκτρος, *amber.* ἄμμος, *sand.* ψάμαθος, *sand.* ἄσβολος, *soot.* βῶλος, *clod.* ὕαλος, *glass.* κόπρος, *dung.* γύψος, *chalk.*	Names of *earths* and *stones*, like ψῆφος, ψάμμος, πλίνθος, σποδός, βάσανος.

And others.

NOTE.—ὁ λίθος, *stone*, but ἡ λίθος, of some particular stone, like the diamond; ὁ κρύσταλλος, *ice*, ἡ κρύσταλλος, *crystal.*

Other words are merely Feminine Adjectives, the Substantives originally attached to them having dropped off; as—

ἡ αὔλειος (θύρα), *the house-door.*
ἡ διάλεκτος (φωνή), *dialect.*
ἡ σύγκλητος (ἐκκλησία) *Senate.*
ἡ διάμετρος (γραμμή), *diameter.*
ἡ ἄνυδρος (χώρα), *desert.*
ἡ βάρβαρος (γῆ), *foreign land.*
ἡ περίχωρος (γῆ), *neighbourhood.*

And others.

23. **Third Declension.**—Masculine without exception are all Substantives in ᾱν, ᾱς (Gen. αντος), ευς and ῡν; as, ὁ παιάν, *chant* (Gen. παιᾶνος); ὁ ἱμάς, *thong* (Gen. ἱμάντος); ὁ στροφεύς, *socket* (Gen. στροφέως); ὁ μόσσῡν, *wooden tower.*

Masculine are words in ην, ηρ, ης, ειρ, ους; ων (Gen. ωνος *and* οντος), ωρ, ως (Gen. ωτος and ωος); as, ὁ σωλήν, *channel*

(Gen. σωλῆνος); ὁ αὐχήν, *neck* (Gen. αὐχένος); ὁ σπινθήρ, *spark* (Gen. σπινθῆρος); ὁ ἀστήρ, *star* (Gen. ἀστέρος); ὁ λέβης, *caldron* (Gen. λέβητος); ὁ φθείρ, *louse* (Gen. φθειρός); ὁ πλακοῦς, *cake* (Gen. πλακοῦντος); ὁ πούς, *foot* (Gen. ποδός); ὁ χοῦς, *a liquid measure* (Gen. χοός); ὁ κλών, *twig* (Gen. κλωνός); ὁ τένων, *sinew* (Gen. τένοντος); ὁ φώρ, *thief* (Gen. φωρός); ὁ ἄχωρ, *scurf* (Gen. ἄχορος); ὁ ἔρως, *love* (Gen. ἔρωτος); ὁ δμώς, *slave* (Gen. δμωός).

Exceptions :—

ην	Feminine φρήν, *heart* (Gen. φρενός).
ηρ	Feminine κήρ, *doom*, Neuter κῆρ, *heart*.
ης	Feminine are all Abstract Nouns, as, ταχυτής, *speed* (Gen. ταχυτῆτος). Add to these ἐσθής, *raiment* (Gen. ἐσθῆτος).
ειρ, ους . .	Feminine χείρ, *hand* (Gen. χειρός).
	Neuter οὖς, *ear* (Gen. ὠτός).
ων	Feminine κώδων, *bell* (Gen. κώδωνος).
	Common αὐλών *defile, channel* (Gen. αὐλῶνος).
ωρ	Neuter σκῶρ, *dirt* (Gen. σκατός); ὕδωρ, *water* (Gen. ὕδατος).
ως	Neuter φῶς, *light* (Gen φωτός).

24. Feminine without exception are Substantives in αυς and ως (Gen. ους), ἡ ναῦς, *ship* (Gen. νεώς); ἡ αἰδώς, *shame* (Gen. αἰδοῦς).

Feminine are Substantives in ας (Gen. ἄδος); εις, ις, υς, and ων (Gen. ονος); as, ἡ λαμπάς, *torch* (Gen. λαμπάδος); ἡ κλείς, *key* (Gen. κλειδός); ἡ μῆνις, *wrath* (Gen. μήνιος); ἡ πόλις, *city* (Gen. πόλεως); ἡ σφραγίς, *seal* (Gen. σφραγῖδος); ἡ χάρις (Gen. χάριτος); ἡ ὠδίς, *pang* (Gen. ὠδῖνος); ἡ ὀφρύς, *eyebrow* (Gen. ὀφρύος); ἡ χλαμύς, *cloak* (Gen. χλαμύδος); ἡ κόρυς, *helmet* (Gen. κόρυθος); ἡ χιών, *snow* (Gen. χιόνος).

Exceptions :—

εις . . .	Masculine κτείς, *comb* (Gen. κτενός).
ις	Masculine are δελφίς, *dolphin* (Gen. δελφῖνος); ἔχις, *adder* (Gen. ἔχεως); ὄφις, *snake* (Gen. ὄφεως).
υς	Masculine are with Genitives in -υος—βότρυς, *grape-cluster*; ἰχθυς, *fish*; μῦς, *mouse*; νέκυς, *dead body*; στάχυς, *ear of corn*. And with Genitives in εως—πῆχυς, *fore-arm*; πέλεκυς, *axe*.
ων . . .	Masculine are ἄκμων, *anvil*; κανών, *rule*. Common κίων, *pillar*.

25. Substantives in ξ are partly Masculine, partly Feminine; those in ψ are Masculine, with the exceptions of ἡ λαῖλαψ, *hurricane* (Gen. λαίλαπος); ἡ φλέψ, *vein* (Gen. φλεβός); ἡ χέρνιψ, *water for the hands* (Gen. χέρνιβος); and the defective ἡ ὄψ, *voice*.

26. Neuter are all Substantives in α, ἄν, ι, εν, ες, ον, ορ, ος, υ; as, τὸ σῶμα, *body* (Gen. σωμάτος); τὸ μέλι, *honey* (Gen. μέλιτος); τὸ σίναπι, *mustard* (Gen. σινάπεως); τὸ ἦτορ, *heart* (defective); τὸ ὄρος, *mountain* (Gen. ὄρους); τὸ ἄστυ, *city* (Gen. ἄστεως).

Neuter are all words in αρ, ας (Gen. ἄτος, ως); as, ἔαρ, *spring* (Gen. ἦρος); νέκταρ, *nectar* (Gen. νέκτᾰρος); ἧπαρ, *liver* (Gen. ἥπατος); κέρας, *horn* (Gen. κέρᾱτος, κέρως); κρέας, *flesh* (Gen. κρέως).

Exceptions :—

αρ . . .	Masculine ψάρ, *starling* (Gen. ψᾱρός).
ας . . .	Masculine λᾶς, *stone* (Gen. λᾶος).

CHAPTER V.

ACCENTUATION.

27. Of the three marks of accent mentioned on p. 72 the Grave is not written in Greek except when it represents a subdued Acute. Thus in the sentence οὗτος ἔδησε τὸν ἵππον (*he tied the horse*), the word τόν has the Grave accent simply because there is no pause immediately after it sufficient to allow of its receiving the full force of the Acute. But οὗτος, ἔδησε, and ἵππον have really the Grave accent on those syllables not already accented, and might be written οὗτὸς, ἔδὴσὲ, ἵππὸν.

28. The Acute can stand upon any one of the three last, the Circumflex upon either of the two last syllables. A word is called Oxytone, Perispomenon, or Barytone, according as the last syllable has the Acute, the Circumflex, or neither. A word having the Acute upon the last syllable but one is called Paroxytone, upon the last but two Proparoxytone; *e.g.*, ἵππος is Paroxytone, ἔδησε Proparoxytone. A word having the Circumflex upon the last syllable but one is called Properispomenon, as οὗτος.

29. The Acute may be on long or short syllables, the Circumflex only on such syllables as are long by nature.

The Acute accent can be on the last syllable but two only if the last is short, as εὔμορφος, but not εὔμορφου.

The Circumflex can be on the last but one only if the last be short by nature, as σῦκον, but not σῦκου.

The diphthongs αι and οι are treated as short, as ἄνθρωποι, μοῦσαι, and if the last syllable is long by position it *does not* prevent the preceding syllable from having the *Circumflex*.

A last syllable but one when long by nature, if accented at all, must have the Circumflex whenever the last syllable is short by nature, as ἧγον, not ἥγον, γυναῖκες, not γυναίκες.

Exceptions like ὧστε are only apparent. See *infra*, § 35 (4) *Obs.*

30. The accent of a word is altered by the changes which a word undergoes in inflexion, contraction, &c.

No syllable acquires an accent from the mere fact of contraction.

A contracted final syllable has the Circumflex if the first of the uncontracted syllables was accented, as, τιμάει, τιμᾷ, χρυσέου, χρυσοῦ; but the Acute if the last was accented, as γεγαώς, γεγώς.

31. When an Oxytone word undergoes Elision, if a Preposition or a Conjunction it loses its accent altogether, but in all other cases throws it back upon the previous syllable, as παρ' ἐμοῦ for παρὰ ἐμοῦ, οὐδ' ἐγώ for οὐδὲ ἐγώ, but δείν' ἔπη (for δεινὰ ἔπη).

32. In the case of Crasis, the accent of the first word disappears, as τἀγαθά for τὰ ἀγαθά. But if the second word is Paroxytone, and its accented syllable becomes through Crasis long by nature, that syllable acquires the Circumflex, as τἆργα for τὰ ἔργα.

33. When placed after the word to which they belong all dissyllabic Prepositions except ἀμφί, ἀντί, ἀνά, διά, throw their accent back on to their first syllable, as κακῶν ἄπο for ἀπὸ κακῶν.

34. As in Latin we find some words which always adhere to the word which precedes them, so in Greek there are certain words which have so little individuality that they *throw their accent* on to the preceding word. These Greek *equivalents of the* Latin *-que*, *nĕ*, &c., are called Enclitics, *and are as follows :—*

(1) All the forms of the Indefinite Pronoun τις, τι (see p. 42), and the Indefinite Adverbs που, ποι, πη, πως, ποθεν, πω, ποτε.

(2) The Particles γε, τε, νυν, περ, τοι, and δε (meaning *towards*, and always attached to the preceding word).

(3) Of the Personal Pronouns the forms με, μου, μοι, and also (unless emphatic, or after a Preposition) σε, σου, σοι, ἑ, οἱ, σφε, σφιν, σφισι(ν).

(4) The Present Indicative of εἰμί (except in the Second Person Singular), unless it be emphatic, or stand at the beginning of a clause, or follow ἀλλά, οὐκ, μή, εἰ, ὡς, καί, τοῦτο. In these cases ἔστι is always Paroxytone, as ἔστι γὰρ οὕτως, μεῖζον οὐκ ἔστι κακόν, &c.

35. Enclitics throw their accent back on the preceding word in the following way :—

(1) A preceding Oxytone does not subdue its accent to the Grave, as καλόν τι, *something beautiful.*

(2) After a Perispome the accent of the Enclitic is entirely lost, as καλῶς τε, *and beautifully.*

(3) After a Paroxytone, Enclitics of one syllable lose their accent, Enclitics of two syllables retain their accent on their last syllable, as, λόγος τις, *a certain speech*, but λόγοι τινές, *some speeches.*

(4) Proparoxytones and Properispomes receive from a following Enclitic an additional accent on their last syllable, as, δεῖξόν μοι, *show me;* ἄνθρωπός τις, *a certain man.*

Observation.—By these rules are explained such apparent exceptions to § 29 as ὥστε for ὥς τε, ὥσπερ for ὥς περ, &c.

(5) When several Enclitics follow one another each throws its accent upon the preceding, as εἴ τίς μοί φησί ποτε, *If any one ever says to me.*

36. Certain words have no accent. These are :—

(1) Of the Article the forms ὁ, ἡ, οἱ, αἱ.

(2) The Prepositions ἐν, ἐς, or εἰς, ὡς, ἐκ, or ἐξ.

(3) The Conjunctions εἰ and ὡς.

(4) The Negative οὐ, οὐκ, or οὐχ.

These may be accented, but only when they are at the end of a sentence or precede an Enclitic, as φῂς ἢ οὔ; *do you say so or not?* οὔ φησι, *he denies.*

37. The accent of words changes with inflection. In regard to Nouns and Adjectives, the principal rule is—Knowing the accent of the Nominative Singular, accent the other cases on the same syllable if the last syllable permits; otherwise accent the following syllable. Exceptions to this rule will be given as they occur.

38. But Verbs throw their accent as far back as the last syllable permits, with this reservation, that in Compound Verbs the accent must not precede the Augment, λύομεν, λελύκαμεν, ἐλέλυντο, but παρέσχον, not πάρεσχον, παρεῖχον, not πάρειχον.

The main exceptions to this rule are these:—

(1) Accented on the penult, the First Aorist Active Infinitive, the Second Aorist Middle Infinitive, the Perfect Middle Infinitive and Participle, τιμῆσαι, πιθέσθαι, λελύσθαι, λελυμένος.

(2) Oxytone are the Second Aorist Participle Active; Participles in εις, ους, υς, ως, and *Present* Participles in -ας, as πιθών, λυθείς, διδούς, δεικνύς, λελυκώς, ἱστάς (but λύσας).

(3) Perispomena are the Second Aorist Active Infinitive, and (except in Verbs compounded with a dissyllabic Preposition) the Second Person Singular, Second Aorist Imperative Middle, as πιθεῖν, πιθοῦ, προδοῦ, but παραλάβου.

Observation 1.—Participles in their inflexion are accented as Nouns, not as Verbs.

Observation 2.—The diphthongs αι and οι are in the *Optative Mood* regarded as long, not as short.

CHAPTER VI.

§§ X.—XV.

FIRST DECLENSION.

39. Of the words you have already learned, Ἑρμῆς is really a contracted form of an older Ἑρμέας. There are also a few Feminine Nouns contracted in the same way, as συκῆ, *fig-tree*, for συκέα.

N. V.	συκῆ.
A.	συκῆν.
G.	συκῆς.
D.	συκῇ.

But a few contract the εα into α, which they retain throughout, as μνᾶ, *mina* (*an Athenian coin*), for μνέα, βορρᾶς, *north wind*, for βορέας.

N.	μνᾶ.	βορρᾶς.
V.	μνᾶ.	βορρᾶ.
A.	μνᾶν.	βορρᾶν.
G.	μνᾶς.	βορρᾶ.
D.	μνᾷ.	βορρᾷ.

The Plural is always the same whether for Masculine or Feminine, for contracted or uncontracted Nouns.

40. The Dative Plural was originally formed by adding ισι to the stem, as, stem τιμα, Dat. Plural τιμα-ισι, and this longer form you will find in Attic poetry, and occasionally in elevated prose.

The Genitive Plural was formed by adding *-ων* to the stem, as *τιμά-ων*, which became by contraction *τιμῶν*. It is due to this fact that all Nouns of the First Declension have the Circumflex on the last syllable of their Genitive Plural. Adjectives do not follow this rule, and two Substantives are exceptions, namely, *χρήστης*, *a usurer*, G. Pl. *χρήστων*, and *ἐτησίαι*, *trade-winds*, G. Pl. *ἐτησίων*.

41. *Additional Examples for Practice.*

FEMININE.

θύρα, *door.*
ἡμέρα, *day.*
πλευρά, *side.*
δορά, *hide.*
μοῖρα, *fate.*
γέφυρα, *bridge.*
μάχαιρα, *sword.*
δωρεά, *present.*
φιλία, *friendship.*
εὔνοια, *goodwill.*
παιδεία, *education.*
στρατεία, *expedition.*

δόξα, *opinion.*
θάλασσα, *sea.*
τράπεζα, *table.*
ἄκανθα, *thorn.*
μέριμνα, *care.*
θεράπαινα, *handmaid.*
λέαινα, *lioness.*
δίψα, *thirst.*
χλαῖνα, *cloak.*
ἅμιλλα, *struggle.*
δίαιτα, *way of life.*
ἔχιδνα, *adder.*

μάχη, *fight.*
τροφή, *nurture.*
ψυχή, *soul.*
πύλη, *gate.*
λύπη, *pain.*
κλίνη, *bed.*
στήλη, *pillar.*
ἀρέτη, *virtue.*
μορφή, *form.*
ἀξίνη, *axe.*
κώμη, *village.*
κόμη, *hair.*

MASCULINE.

νεανίας, *young-man.*
βορέας, *north wind.*
Λοξίας, *Loxias.*
προδότης, *traitor.*
ποιητής, *poet.*
μαθητής, *scholar.*
στρατιώτης, *soldier.*
...της, *master.*

κλέπτης, *thief.*
τεχνίτης, *artificer.*
εὐεργέτης, *benefactor.*
λῃστής, *robber.*
ὁπλίτης, *heavy-armed soldier.*
βουλευτής, *councillor.*
ἀθλητής, *champion.*

CONTRACTED.

γῆ, *earth.*	μνᾶ, *mina.*
γαλῆ, *weasel.*	Ἀθηνᾶ (*the goddess*) *Athena.*
λεοντῆ, *lion's skin.*	βορρᾶς, *north wind.*

42. If you examine the above examples you will find—

(1) That α remains in the Nominative Singular after ε, ι, ρ, σ, ζ, ξ, ψ, σσ, λλ, and in the Feminine designation αινα. Exceptions are κόρη, *girl*, κόρρη, *temple* (*of the head*), ἕρση, *dew.*

(2) That after all other letters, whether vowels or consonants, α is changed to η. Exceptions are στοά, *colonnade;* χρόα, *colour;* τόλμα, *boldness;* δίαιτα, *way of life;* μέριμνα, *care;* ἔχιδνα, *adder.*

SECOND DECLENSION.

43. The Dative Plural was originally formed by adding ισι to the stem, as λογο-ισι. This longer form you will find in Attic poetry, and sometimes even in prose.

44. *Additional Examples for Practice.*

ὁ πόνος, *labour.*	τὸ μέτρον, *measure.*
χρόνος, *time.*	δεῖπνον, *meal-time.*
δῆμος, *people.*	πεδίον, *plain.*
οἶκος, *house.*	ἔργον, *work.*
πλοῦτος, *wealth.*	δῶρον, *present.*
ὀφθαλμός, *eye.*	ζυγόν, *yoke.*
ἵππος, *horse.*	τόξον, *bow.*
ἀριθμός, *number.*	χωρίον, *place.*
ποταμός, *river.*	πτερόν, *wing.*
πόλεμος, *war.*	ἱμάτιον, *garment.*

For Feminine Nouns, see page 81, § 22.

CONTRACTED.

ὁ χνοῦς, *foam.* ὁ ἀνεψιαδοῦς, *second cousin.*
ῥοῦς, *stream.* θυγατριδοῦς, *daughter's son.*
νοῦς, *mind.* τὸ κανοῦν, *basket.*

In these contracted words there are some irregularities of accent, namely—

(1) The Nom. Acc. and Voc. Dual are made Oxytone, contrary to § 30.

(2) Compound words have the accent on the last syllable but one, contrary to § 30; as, εἴσπλῳ for εἰσπλόῳ.

ATTIC DECLENSION.

45. The forms like νεώς and ἀνώγεων have been called Attic. Additional examples are—

ὁ λαγώς, *hare.*
λεώς, *people.*
Ἄθως, *Mount Athos.*
Μίνως, *Minos.*
ἡ ἅλως, *threshing-floor.*
Κέως, *Ceos (island).*
Κώς, *Cos (island).*
ἕως, *dawn.*

Of these words all but λεώς may have their Accusative in ω, and ἕως always has; as λαγών or λαγώ, but λεών and ἕω.

46. The accentuation is irregular: (1) εω passes as one syllable as regards accent; (2) in the Genitive and Dative the last syllable when accented has the Acute, in violation of the rule that, *In Genitives and Datives of all Numbers a long final syllable when accented takes the Circumflex.*

CHAPTER VII.

§§ XVI. ff.

THIRD DECLENSION.

47. WORDS belonging to this Declension violate the general rules of accentuation in this, that words of one syllable accentuate the Genitive and Dative of all numbers on the case-ending, as, πούς, *foot*, ποδός, ποδί, ποδοῖν, ποδῶν, ποσί.

Exceptions to this are—

(1) The nine words, παῖς, *boy*; δμώς, *slave*; δᾴς, *torch*; σής, *moth*; οὖς, *ear*; Τρώς, *Trojan*; θώς, *jackal*; τὸ φώς, *light*; ἡ φῷς, *blister*; which are Paroxytones in the Genitive and Dative Dual and Plural. The Adjective πᾶς has the same peculiarity, παντός, παντί; but πάντων, πᾶσι(ν).

(2) Monosyllabic Participles accent the Genitive and Dative of all numbers on the last syllable but one, as, δούς, *giving*, Gen. δόντος, ὤν, *being*, Gen. ὄντος.

GUTTURAL AND LABIAL STEMS.

48. *Additional Examples for Practice.*

STEMS IN κ.	STEMS IN γ.
ὁ θώραξ, *breastplate.*	ὁ κόκκυξ, *cuckoo.*
κόραξ, *raven.*	ὄρτυξ, *quail.*
σφήξ, *wasp.*	τέττιξ, *grasshopper.*
φοῖνιξ, *palm-tree.*	ἡ φλόξ, *flame.*
κῆρυξ, *herald.*	πτέρυξ, *wing.*
ἡ κύλιξ, *beaker.*	σάλπιγξ, trumpet.
κάλυξ, *husk.*	πέμφιξ, bubble.
σάρξ, *flesh.*	

STEMS IN π.

ὁ λαῖλαψ, *hurricane.*
κώνωψ, *gnat.*

STEMS IN β.

ὁ Ἄραψ, *Arab.*
ἡ χέρνιψ, *water for the hands.*

Stems in χ are rare.

There are no stems in φ except κατηλιφ, Nom. κατῆλιψ, defective, and of uncertain meaning.

Observation.—ἀλώπηξ, *f. fox*, κῆρυξ and φοῖνιξ, from ἀλωπεκ, κηρῡκ and φοινῑκ, are anomalous, the stem vowel being in the first case lengthened, in the others shortened to form the Nominative. The stem τριχ, *f. hair*, forms a Nominative Singular θρίξ, and a Dative Plural θριξί(ν).

STEMS IN DENTALS.

49. *Additional Examples for Practice.*

STEMS IN τ.

ὁ ἱδρώς, *sweat.*
χρώς, *skin.*
κέλης, *riding horse.*
λέβης, *caldron.*
Κρής, *Cretan.*
ἡ δαίς, *meal.*
ἐσθής, *raiment.*
χάρις, *favour.*
γλυκύτης, *sweetness.*
νύξ, *night.*
τὸ ὄνομα, *name.*
χρῆμα, *thing.*
κῦμα, *wave.*
αἴνιγμα, *riddle.*

STEMS IN δ.

ἡ σφραγίς, *seal.*
κρηπίς, *base.*
χλαμύς, *cloak.*
πατρίς, *native land.*

Besides κορυθ and ὀρνιθ there are few stems in θ, and these few not in common use.

There is one Neuter in ιτ, namely, μέλι, *honey*, Gen. μέλιτι.

50. Barytone stems in ιδ, ιτ, ιθ, υθ, υδ, often form the Accusative Singular by affixing ν after rejecting the final consonant of the Stem, as ἔρις, *strife* (stem ἐριδ), Acc. ἔριν, Ἄρτεμις, *Artemis* (Stem Ἀρτεμιδ), Acc. Ἄρτεμιν, χάρις, *favour* (Stem χαριτ), Acc. χάριν or χάριτα, κόρυς, *helmet* (Stem κορυθ), Acc. κόρυν or κόρυθα.

Oxytone words have always α, as ἐλπίς, *hope*, Acc. ἐλπίδα, never ἐλπίν. The Vocative of such words is sometimes different from the Nominative, *e.g.*, τυραννίς, *despotic power* (Stem τυραννιδ), Voc. τυραννί.

DENTAL STEMS IN ντ.

51. *Additional Examples for Practice.*

ὁ ἐλέφας, *elephant.*
ἱμάς, *thong.*
ἀνδρίας, *statue.*
δράκων, *dragon.*
θεράπων, *servant.*

STEMS IN DENTAL ν.

52. *Additional Examples for Practice.*

Like Ἕλλην or ἀγών—
ὁ παιάν, *battle-song.*
κλών, *twig.*
λειμών, *meadow.*
πώγων, *beard.*
χήν, *gander.*
μήν, *month.*
Τιτάν, *Titan.*
Πάν, (*the god*) *Pan.*
χειμών, *winter.*
αἰών, *age.*

Like ποιμήν or ἡγεμών—
ὁ αὐχήν, *neck.*
λιμήν *haven.*
ὁ, ἡ ἀλεκτρυών, *cock, hen.*
ὁ, ἡ γείτων, *neighbour.*
ὁ κανών, *rule.*
ἡ χιών, *snow.*
εἰκών, *image.*

Like δελφίς—
ἡ ἀκτίς, *ray.*
ὠδίς, *pang.*

53. The words Ποσειδῶν, Ἀπόλλων not only shorten their stem in the Vocative, but also elide ν in the Accusative and contract, as Ποσειδῶ, Ἀπόλλω for Ποσειδῶνα and Ἀπόλλωνα. As a rule the shorter forms are confined to adjurations, as νὴ τὸν Ἀπόλλω. The accent is drawn back in the Vocatives Ἄπολλον and Πόσειδον, and in a few others, as, Ἀγάμεμνον.

STEMS IN LIQUID ρ.

54. *Additional Examples for Practice.*

Like θήρ—
ὁ ζωστήρ, *girdle.*
ψάρ, *starling.*
φώρ, *thief.*
πάνθηρ, *panther.*
Κάρ, *Carian.*
θηρητήρ, *hunter.*

Like ῥήτωρ—
ὁ ἀήρ, *air (no Plural).*
πράκτωρ, *doer.*
αἰθήρ, *ether (no Plural).*
μητροπάτωρ, *mother's father.*

ὁ ἀστήρ, *star,* is declined like αἰθήρ, but the Dative Plural has ἀστράσι(ν) by metathesis.

STEMS IN SOFT VOWELS.

55. *Additional Examples for Practice.*

Like πόλις—
ἡ φύσις, *nature.*
ποίησις, *making.*
δύναμις, *power.*
ὕβρις, *insolence.*
στάσις, *faction.*
ὁ ὄφις, *snake.*
μάντις, *seer.*

Like σῦς—
ὁ μῦς, *mouse.*
βότρυς, *grape-cluster.*
στάχυς, *ear of corn.*
ἰχθῦς, *fish.*
ἡ δρῦς, *oak tree.*
ὀφρῦς, *brow.*

56. Like πῆχυς are declined, ὁ πέλεκυς, *axe;* πρέσβυς, *old man;* and the Plural of ἡ ἔγχελυς, *eel.*

N. πέλεκυς.	N. A. πελέκεε (κη).	N. πελέκεις.
A. πέλεκυν.	G. D. πελεκέοιν.	A. πελέκεις.
G. πελέκεως.		G. πελέκεων.
D. πελέκει.		D. πελέκεσι.

N. πρέσβυς.	N. A. πρέσβεε (η).	N. πρέσβεις.
V. πρέσβυ.		V. πρέσβεις.
A. πρέσβυν.	G. D. πρεσβέοιν.	A. πρέσβεις.
G. πρέσβεως.		G. πρέσβεων.
D. πρέσβει.		D. πρέσβεσι.

The Singular is only used in poetry, but the Dual and Plural have in prose the meaning of *ambassadors,* for the Singular of which πρεσβευτής is used.

N. ἔγχελυς.	ἐγχέλεις.
A. ἔγχελυν.	ἐγχέλεις.
G. ἐγχέλυος.	ἐγχέλεων.
D. ἐγχέλυι.	ἐγχέλεσι.

Observe the fact that the long final syllable in the Genitive Singular and Plural of soft vowel stems does not prevent the accent from being on the antepenult.

57. Neuters of this class are very rare, ἄστυ being the only fully-declined word in common use. The Genitive of ἄστυ is generally given as ἄστεος, but in favour of ἄστεως is the fact that there are many lines in poetry which require ἄστεως, but none in which ἄστεος must be read. Other words, like νᾶπυ, *mustard,* only occur in the Nominative and Accusative Singular. There are in Attic no Neuters *ending in* ι.

STEMS IN ευ, αυ, ου.

58. Stems which have a vowel before ευ are contracted, not only in the Dative Singular and the Nominative Plural, but also in the Genitive and the Accusative Singular and Plural, as, Ἐρετριευ, *a dweller in Eretria.*

N.	Ἐρετριεύς.	Ἐρετριεῖς.
V.	Ἐρετριεῦ.	Ἐρετριεῖς.
A.	Ἐρετριᾶ.	Ἐρετριᾶς.
G.	Ἐρετριῶς.	Ἐρετριῶν.
D.	Ἐρετριεῖ.	Ἐρετριεῦσι(ν).

59. *Additional Examples for Practice.*

ὁ ἱππεύς, *horseman.*
ἱερεύς, *priest.*
γραφεύς, *painter.*
Δωριεύς, *Dorian.*
Εὐβοεύς, *Euboean.*
Πειραιεύς, *Piraeus* (*no Plural*).

There are no other words in general use declined like βοῦς or γραῦς.

60. The Accusative Plural of Masculine stems in ευ ought not to be contracted to -εις or ης. The contracted form does not occur in Attic Comedy—the only true criterion. It is just possible that Xenophon used it, but he often sins against his native tongue.

STEMS IN ο AND ω.

61. As a matter of fact the assigning of a Second *Declension Dual* and Plural to stems in ο is a fiction of grammarians. The words have naturally no plural, and Γοργώ, which has, forms its plural from the stem Γοργον.

Like πειθώ—	Like ἥρως—
ἠχώ, *echo.*	μήτρως, *maternal uncle.*
Λητώ, *Leto.*	πάτρως, *paternal uncle.*
Ἰώ, *Io.*	

STEMS WHICH ELIDE σ.

62. Proper names in κλέης contract in all cases, and doubly in the Dative Singular, as Ἡρακλέης, *Heracles* (*the hero*).

N. Ἡρακλῆς.
V. Ἡρακλεῖς.
A. Ἡρακλέā.
G. Ἡρακλέους.
D. Ἡρακλεῖ.

When proper names like Δημοσθένης require a Plural, they take the First Declension forms, as οἱ Ἀριστοφάναι in Plato, *Sympos.* 218, B.

63. *Additional Examples for Practice.*

ὁ Σωκράτης, *Socrates.*
Σοφοκλῆς, *Sophocles.*
τὸ ὄρος, *mountain.*
ἄνθος, *flower.*
ψεῦδος, *lie.*
ἔθνος, *nation.*
τεῖχος, *wall.*

STEMS WHICH ELIDE τ.

64. *Κέρας* stands alone in Attic. The uncontracted forms are by far the more frequent—except in the phrase

ἐπὶ κέρως, referring to military evolutions. τέρας, *prodigy*, Gen. τέρᾰτος, never contracts at all in Attic.

There are many defective words which, when found, follow the same Declension as κρέας, such as γέρας, *prerogative*, Gen. γέρως, Nom. Plural γέρα, Gen. γερῶν, Dat. γέρᾰσι.

γῆρας, *old age*, Gen. γήρως, Dat. γήρᾳ.

σέλας, *splendour*, Nom. and Acc. Sing.

σέβας, *object of wonder*, Nom. and Acc. Sing.

κνέφας, *dawn*, Dat. κνέφᾳ, Gen. κνέφους (as if from κνέφος).

CHAPTER VIII.

§§ XXXII., ff.

65. THERE are also some contracted Adjectives with only two terminations, as εὔνους, εὔνουν, *well-disposed*, εὔπνους, *airy*, εὔρρους, *fluent*. They have this peculiarity, that they do not contract their Nominative or Accusative Plural Neuter, *e.g.*, εὔπλοα (not εὔπλα) εὔπνοα, εὔρροα.

66. Like ἵλεως are declined ἀγήρως, *exempt from old age*, ἀξιόχρεως, *substantial*, and a few others, among which are the compounds of πλέως, *full*, as ἀνάπλεως, περίπλεως, ἔμπλεως. The simple πλέως is itself irregular.

	SINGULAR.			PLURAL.	
N. πλέως.	πλέα.	πλέων.	πλέῳ.	πλέαι.	πλέα.
A. πλέων.	πλέαν.	πλέων.	πλέως.	πλέας.	πλέα.
G. πλέω.	πλέας.	πλέω.		πλέων.	
D. πλέῳ.	πλέᾳ.	πλέῳ.	πλέῳς.	πλέαις.	πλέῳς.

For σῶς, *safe*, see, *infra*, p. 103, § 74.

67. Like ἡδύς are declined γλυκύς, *sweet;* εὐρύς, *broad;* βραχύς, *short;* ταχύς, *swift;* θῆλυς, *feminine;* and others.

Unlike Substantives, Adjectives do not contract εα, as ἄστη, but ἡδέα.

The compounds of πῆχυς are exceptions to this rule, as διπήχη, τριπήχη, &c., not διπήχεα, τριπήχεα.

Like μέλας is declined τάλας, τάλαινα, τάλαν, *wretched.*

68. There are many Adjectives like χαρίεις, but they are rare in Attic, νιφόεις, *snowy;* ὑλήεις, *wooded;* πτερόεις, *winged.* Those in -οεις were occasionally contracted, as πτεροῦς, πτεροῦσσα, πτεροῦν. The Substantives ὁ πλακοῦς, *flat-cake,* and ἡ μελιτοῦττα, *honey-cake,* are really the contracted Masculine and Feminine respectively of the Adjectives πλακόεις and μελιοττόεις.

69. In Adjectives like εὐγενής, if the ης of the Nominative is preceded by a vowel, εα contracts to α, not to η, as ὑγιής, *healthy* (stem ὑγιεσ).

SINGULAR.			PLURAL.		
N.	ὑγιής.	ὑγιές	N.A.V.	ὑγιεῖς.	ὑγιᾶ.
V.	ὑγιές.		G.	ὑγιῶν.	
A.	ὑγιᾶ.	ὑγιές.	D.	ὑγιέσι.	
G.	ὑγιοῦς.		DUAL.		
D.	ὑγιεῖ.		N.A.V.	ὑγιῆ.	
			G.D.	ὑγιοῖν.	

But forms in η are occasionally found.

Barytone Adjectives have the accent in the Genitive Plural on the last syllable but one, contrary to p. 86, § 30, as συνήθων for συνηθέων.

70. *Additional examples for Practice.*

σαφής, *clear.* εὐώδης, fragrant.
εὐτελής, *cheap.* ἐπιφανής, notable.
αὐθάδης, *self-willed.* εὐήθης, simple.

αὐτάρκης, *self-sufficient.*	ἐνδεής, *deficient in.*
εὐφυής, *well-made.*	ὑποδεής, *inferior.*
τριήρης, *triply-fitted.*	εὐδαίμων, *prosperous.*
ἡδίων, *sweeter.*	πλείων, *more.*

Of these τριήρης is only used in the Feminine (sc. ναῦς, *a trireme*), and πλείων is somewhat irregular.

SINGULAR.

N.	πλείων.	πλεῖον, πλέον, πλεῖν.
A.	πλείονα, πλείω.	πλεῖον, πλέον, πλεῖν.
G.	πλείονος.	
D.	πλείονι.	

PLURAL.

N.	πλείονες, πλείους.	πλείονα, πλείω.
A.	πλείονας, πλείους.	πλείονα, πλείω.
G.	πλειόνων.	
D.	πλείοσι.	

71. Many of the Adjectives of one termination ought rather to be considered as Substantives of Common Gender, as φυγάς, ὁ, ἡ, (stem φυγαδ), *exiled; αὐτοκράτωρ, ὁ, ἡ, plenipotentiary, arbitrary; φιλόπολις, ὁ, ἡ, patriotic;* (stem φιλοπολιδ). Occasionally the poets formed a Neuter even to these, as αὐτοκράτορα. The compounds of χάρις have a Neuter even in prose, as εὔχαρις, ὁ, ἡ, εὔχαρι, τό, *winning.*

	SINGULAR.		PLURAL.	
N.	εὔχαρις.	εὔχαρι.	εὐχάριτες.	εὐχάριτα.
A.	εὔχαριν.	εὔχαρι.	εὐχάριτας.	εὐχάριτα.
G.	εὐχάριτος.		εὐχαρίτων.	
D.	εὐχάριτι.		εὐχάρισι.	

72. The compounds of πούς form a Neuter in -πουν, e.g. ἄπους, *without feet, halt.*

	Singular.		Plural.	
N.	ἄπους.	ἄπουν.	ἄποδες.	ἄποδα.
A.	ἄποδα.	ἄπουν.	ἄποδας.	ἄποδα.
G.	ἄποδος.		ἀπόδων.	
D.	ἄποδι.		ἄποσι.	

Some compounds prefer to form their Accusative Singular Masculine in -πουν, as πουλύπους, *many-footed*, Acc. πουλύπουν.

73. πρᾶος, *gentle*, has some of its forms from a stem πραυ of the third Declension.

Singular.

N.	πρᾶος.	πραεῖα.	πρᾶον.
A.	πρᾶον.	πραεῖαν.	πρᾶον.
G.	πράου.	πραείας.	πράου.
D.	πράῳ.	πραείᾳ.	πράῳ.

Plural.

N.	πρᾶοι.	πραεῖαι.	πραέα.
A.	πράους.	πραείας.	πραέα.
G.	πραέων.	πραειών.	πραέων.
D.	πράοις or πραέσι.	πραείαις.	πράοις or πραέσι.

74. σῶς, *safe*, forms most of its cases from the stem σωο.

Singular.

N.	σῶς.	σώα.	σῶν.
A.	σῶν.	σώαν.	σῶν.
G.	σώου.	σώας.	σώου.
D.	σώῳ.	σώᾳ.	σώῳ.

Plural.

N.	σῶοι or σῶς.	σῶαι.	σῶα or σᾶ.
A.	σώους or σῶς.	σώας.	σῶα or σᾶ.
G.		σώων.	
D.	σώοις.	σώαις.	σώοις.

CHAPTER IX.

§§ XL.—XLIII.

COMPARISON.

75. LIKE γεραιός are παλαιός, *ancient*, and σχολαῖος, *slow*, but, unlike γεραιός, they have also the forms in ο, as παλαιότερος, σχολαιότερος.

76. Like μέσος, ἴσος, and εὔδιος, we also find πλήσιος, *near;* ἥσυχος, *at rest;* φίλος, *dear;* ὄψιος, *late;* and πρῷος, *early;* but ἴδιος, *private*, which is often added, never so forms its Comparative and Superlative in Attic Greek.

πλησιαίτερος.	πλησιαίτατος.
ἡσυχαίτερος.	ἡσυχαίτατος.
φιλαίτερος.	φιλαίτατος.
ὀψιαίτερος.	ὀψιαίτατος.
πρῳαίτερος.	πρῳαίτατος.

ἥσυχος may also have ἡσυχώτερος, ἡσυχώτατος.

φίλτερος is poetical, but φίλτατος is by far the more common Superlative form. The forms φιλώτερος, φιλώτατος do not occur except once in Xenophon in a play upon words.

77. Of Adjectives in -ων, the words πίων, *fat*, and πέπων, *ripe*, form their Comparative and Superlative irregularly.

πίων.	πιότερος.	πιότατος.
πέπων.	πεπαίτερος.	πεπαίτατος.

78. Like ἄκρατος are compared ἐρρωμένος, *strong*, ἐπίπεδος, *el*, and sometimes ἄφθονος, *abundant*.

ἐρρωμενέστερος.	ἐρρωμενέστατος.
ἐπιπεδέστερος.	ἐπιπεδέστατος.
ἀφθονώτερος,	ἀφθονώτατος,
or έστερος.	or έστατος.

79. The words ὑβριστής, *insolent* (*man*), and ἐπίχαρις, *charming*, form their Comparative and Superlative as if from ὑβριστός and ἐπιχάριτος.

ὑβριστότερος.	ὑβριστότατος.
ἐπιχαριτώτερος.	ἐπιχαριτώτατος.

80. Of Comparatives and Superlatives formed from Adverbial, Prepositional, or Indeclinable Positives, the following are of most frequent occurrence—

ὑπέρτερος, *upper, further*; ὑπέρτατος, *uppermost* (from prep. ὕπερ, *over*).

ὕστερος, *latter, later*; ὕστατος, *last, latest* (perhaps from ὑπό, *under*).

προὐργιαίτερος, *more serviceable*; προὐργιαίτατος, *most serviceable* (from προὔργου, ὁ, ἡ, τό).

ἔσχατος, *extreme* (perhaps from ἐκ, ἐξ).

81. As in all languages, there are in Greek many Adjectives, which for euphonic or other reasons do not form their Comparatives and Superlatives by inflexional change. These generally use μᾶλλον and μάλιστα, as *magis* and *maxime* are used in Latin; as μᾶλλον δῆλος, *more plain*, δῆλος μάλιστα, or μάλιστα δῆλος, *most plain*.

CHAPTER X.

§ XLIV.

ADVERBS.

82. THERE are many Adverbs besides those formed from Adjectives. They may be formed from Substantival or Verbal stems, and many are of a formation now difficult to trace. Some are simply cases of Adjectives or Nouns. Thus in forms like φίλως we really see the remnants of the Ablative Case in Greek, as in οἴκοι, *at home*, we see the Locative Case of οἶκος, *house*. The Dative supplies a great number, as—

δημοσίᾳ, *publicly*, from δημόσιος, *public*.
ἰδίᾳ, *privately*, from ἴδιος, *private*.
σπουδῇ, *zealously*, from σπουδή, *zeal*.

83. Some are formed from Substantive Stems by the suffix -δον, as κυνηδόν, *like a dog*, and a great number from Verbal Stems by the suffixes -δην and τι, as φύρδην, *mixedly*, from φύρω, *I mix*, ἑλληνιστί, *in Greek*, from Ἑλληνίζω, *I speak Greek*. Others are really phrases like the English *at random*, as ἐκποδών, *out of the way* (for ἐκ ποδῶν).

84. For a large class no general principle of formation can be given. Such are ἅλις, *enough*; αὖθις, *again*; πάλιν, *back*; αὐτίκα, *immediately*; ἐκεῖ, *there*.

85. But many Adverbs of place are formed by the three *suffixes* -ι, -θεν (attached to the Stem or the modified *Stem), and* -δε (attached to the Accusative), as οἴκοι, at *home*, οἴκοθεν, *from home*, and οἰκόνδε, *to home*, from οἶκος, *house*.

Vhen -δε is added to the Accusative Plural it combines ith the σ to form -ζε, as Ἀθήναζε, *to Athens* (for Ἀθήναςδε).

86. The chief Adverbs of time are πότε, *when?* ὁπότε, *when?* (indirect), τότε, *then*, ὅτε, *when*.

CHAPTER XI.

§§ XLVI.—LIV.

87. The Cardinal, Ordinal, and Adverbial Numerals are s follows—

Sign.		Cardinal.	Ordinal.	Adverb.
1	α′	εἷς, μία, ἕν, *one*	ὁ πρῶτος, *the first*	ἅπαξ, *once*
2	β′	δύο	δεύτερος	δίς
3	γ′	τρεῖς, τρία	τρίτος	τρίς
4	δ′	τέσσἄρες τέσσἄρα, or τέττἄρες, τέττἄρα	τέταρτος	τετράκις
5	ε′	πέντε	πέμπτος	πεντάκις
6	ϛ′	ἕξ	ἕκτος	ἑξάκις
7	ζ′	ἑπτά	ἕβδομος	ἑπτάκις
8	η′	ὀκτώ	ὄγδοος	ὀκτάκις
9	θ′	ἐννέα	ἔνατος (ἔννατος)	ἐνάκις (ἐννάκις)
10	ι′	δέκα	δέκατος	δεκάκις
11	ια′	ἕνδεκα	ἑνδέκατος	ἑνδεκάκις
12	ιβ′	δώδεκα	δωδέκατος	δωδεκάκις
13	ιγ′	τρισκαίδεκα	τρισκαιδέκατος	
14	ιδ′	τεσσαρεσκαίδεκα / τεσσαρακαίδεκα	τεσσαρακαιδέκατος	
15	ιε′	πεντεκαίδεκα	πεντεκαιδέκατος	
16	ιϛ′	ἑκκαίδεκα	ἑκκαιδέκατος	
17	ιζ′	ἑπτακαίδεκα	ἑπτακαιδέκατος	
18	ιη′	ὀκτωκαίδεκα	ὀκτωκαιδέκατος	
19	ιθ′	ἐννεακαίδεκα	ἐννεακαιδέκατος	
20	κ′	εἴκοσι(ν)	εἰκοστός	εἰκοσάκις
25	κε′	εἴκοσι πέντε	εἰκοστὸς πέμπτος	εἰκοσάκις πεντάκις

Sign.		Cardinal.	Ordinal.	Adverb.
30	λ'	τριάκοντα	τριᾱκοστός	τριᾱκοντάκις
40	μ'	τεσσαράκοντα	τεσσαρᾰκοστός	τεσσαρᾰκοντάκις
50	ν'	πεντήκοντα	πεντηκοστός	πεντηκοντάκις
60	ξ'	ἑξήκοντα	ἑξηκοστός	ἑξηκοντάκις
70	ο'	ἑβδομήκοντα	ἑβδομηκοστός	ἑβδομηκοντάκις
80	π'	ὀγδοήκοντα	ὀγδοηκοστός	ὀγδοηκοντάκις
90	ϟ'	ἐνενήκοντα	ἐνενηκοστός	ἐνενηκοντάκις
100	ρ'	ἑκατόν	ἑκατοστός	ἑκατοντάκις
200	σ'	διᾱκόσιοι, αι, α	διακοσιοστός	διακοσιάκις
300	τ'	τριᾱκόσιοι, αι, α	τριακοσιοστός	
400	υ'	τετρᾰκόσιοι, αι, α	τετρακοσιοστός	
500	φ'	πεντᾰκόσιοι, αι, α	πεντακοσιοστός	
600	χ'	ἑξᾰκόσιοι, αι, α	ἑξακοσιοστός	
700	ψ'	ἑπτᾰκόσιοι, αι, α	ἑπτακοσιοστός	
800	ω'	ὀκτακόσιοι, αι, α	ὀκτακοσιοστός	
900	ϡ	ἐνᾰκόσιοι, αι, α ἐννᾰκόσιοι, αι, α	ἐνακοσιοστός ἐννακοσιοστός	
1000	͵α	χίλιοι, αι, α	χιλιοστός	χιλιάκις
2000	͵β	δισχίλιοι, αι, α	δισχιλιοστός	
3000	͵γ	τρισχίλιοι, αι, α	τρισχιλιοστός	
10000	͵ι	μύριοι, αι, α	μυριοστός	μυριάκις

88. The letters of the Alphabet were used, as is shown in the second column, as signs of the numbers. To form compound numbers καί was often used, in which case the smaller number was put first, as εἴκοσιν ἕξ, *twenty-six*, but ἓξ καὶ εἴκοσι. So εἰκοστος ἕκτος, but ἕκτος καὶ εἰκοστός. Compounds of 8 or 9 are often expressed by means of the participles of δέω, *I lack*, as δυοῖν δέοντα τριάκοντα, *thirty lacking two*, *i.e.*, *twenty-eight*, ἑνὸς δέον τριακοστὸν ἔτος, *the thirtieth year save one*, *i.e.*, *the twenty-ninth year.*

89. **Fractions** were expressed in different ways. Fractions with the general formula $\frac{1}{m}$ our *quarter*, *fifth*, &c., were expressed by compounds with μόριον, as τριτημόριον = $\frac{1}{3}$, πεμπτημόριον = $\frac{1}{5}$, &c. Fractions with the formula $\frac{n}{m}$ were

expressed by phrases like *τῶν πέντε τὰ τρία μέρη* = $\frac{3}{5}$, *τῶν ἕπτα αἱ δύο μοῖραι* = $\frac{2}{7}$. Fractions with the general formula $\frac{m-1}{m}$ might be expressed as the last, or in a shorter way. Thus *τῶν ἑπτὰ τὰ ἕξ μέρη*, or simply *τὰ ἕξ μέρη* = $\frac{6}{7}$.

90. The most important general Adjectives of quantity are *ἕκαστος*, *each*; *ἑκάτερος*, *either*; *πᾶς*, *all*; *ποστός*, *ὁποστός*, *which in a series?* (Lat. *quotus?*), *πολύς*, *much*; *ὀλίγοι*, *few*. The Adverbs are *ἑκαστάκις*, *every time*; *πολλάκις*, *often*; *πλειστάκις*, *very often*; *ὀλιγάκις*, *seldom*.

91. When *αὐτός* comes between an Article and Substantive it acquires the meaning *same*, as *ὁ αὐτὸς ἀνήρ*, *the same man*. It often coalesces by crasis with those forms of the Article which end in a vowel, as—

SINGULAR.

N.	*αὐτός.*	*αὐτή.*	*ταὐτό, ταὐτόν.*
A.	*τὸν αὐτόν.*	*τὴν αὐτήν.*	*ταὐτό, ταὐτόν.*
G.	*ταὐτοῦ.*	*τῆς αὐτῆς.*	*ταὐτοῦ.*
D.	*ταὐτῷ.*	*ταὐτῇ.*	*ταὐτῷ.*

PLURAL.

N.	*αὐτοί.*	*αὐταί.*	*ταὐτά.*
A.	*τοὺς αὐτούς.*	*τὰς αὐτάς.*	*ταὐτά.*
G.		*τῶν αὐτῶν.*	
D.	*τοῖς αὐτοῖς.*	*ταῖς αὐταῖς.*	*τοῖς αὐτοῖς.*

DUAL.

N. A. V. *ταὐτώ.* G. D. *τοῖν αὐτοῖν.*

92. Like *οὗτος* are declined—

τοσοῦτος.	*τοσαύτη.*	*τοσοῦτο(ν)*, *so great.*
τοιοῦτος.	τοιαύτη.	τοιοῦτο(ν), such.
τηλικοῦτος.	τηλικαύτη.	τηλικοῦτο(ν), so old.

But the τ of the forms of οὗτος beginning in that letter is dropped, as ταῦτα, but τοσ-αῦτα; and the Nominative and Accusative Singular Neuter may end in ν.

With the same meaning as these forms we also find τόσος-δε, τοιός-δε, and τηλίκος-δε declined regularly, except that they have the suffix -δε appended.

93. In the following tables the Pronouns and the Adverbs formed from their Stems are arranged so as best to show their relations to one another.

PRONOMINAL ADJECTIVES.

Interrogative.	Indefinite.	Demonstrative.	Relative.
τίς, *who?*	τὶς, *some one*	ὅδε, οὗτος, *this*	ὅς, ὅστις, *who*
πότερος, *uter? which of two?*	πότερος, *one of two* (*alteruter*)	ἕτερος, *the one of two* (*alter*)	ὁπότερος, *which of two*
πόσος, *how great? how much?* (*quantus, quot*)	ποσός, *of some size or number*	τόσος, τόσοσδε τοσοῦτος, *so great, so much* (*tantus, tot*)	ὅσος, ὁπόσος, *how great, how much* (*quantus, quot*)
ποῖος, *of what quality?* (*qualis*)	ποιός, *of some quality*	τοῖος, τοιόσδε, τοιοῦτος, *of such a quality* (*talis*)	οἷος, ὁποῖος, *of what quality* (*qualis*)
πηλίκος, *how old?*	πηλίκος, *of some age*	τηλίκος, τηλίκοσδε, τηλικοῦτος, *of such age.*	ἡλίκος, ὁπηλίκος, *of what age*

PRONOMINAL ADVERBS.

Interrogative.	Indefinite.	Demonstrative.	Relative.
ποῦ, *where?* (*ubi?*)	που (*alicubi*) } *somewhere*	ἔνθα, ἐνθάδε, ἐνταῦθα } *there* (*ibi*)	οὗ, ὅπου } *where* (*ubi*)
πόθεν, *whence?* (*unde?*)	ποθέν (*alicunde*) } *from somewhere*	ἔνθεν, ἐνθένδε, ἐντεῦθεν } *from there* (*inde*)	ὅθεν, ὁπόθεν } *whence* (*unde*)
ποῖ, *whither?* (*quo?*)	ποί (*aliquo*) } *some whither*	ἔνθα, ἐνθάδε, ἐνταῦθα } *thither* (*eo*)	οἷ, ὅποι } *whither* (*quo*)
πότε, *when?*	ποτέ, *sometime*	τότε, then	ὅτε, ὁπότε, *when*
πηνίκα { *at what time?*		τηνίκα, τηνικάδε, τηνικαῦτα } *at that time*	ἡνίκα, ὁπηνίκα } *at what time*
πῶς, *how?*	πως, *somehow*	ὥς, ὧδε, οὕτως } *thus*	ὡς, ὅπως, *as*
πῇ { *whither? in what way?*	πῃ { *some whither in some way*	τῇδε, ταύτῃ } *thither, in this way.*	ᾗ, ὅπῃ { *whither, in what way*

CHAPTER XII.

§§ LV. ff.

GENERAL REMARKS ON VERBAL FORMS.

94.—Double Forms.

3 Pers. Pl. Imper. Act. λυέτωσαν, λυόντων.
λυσάτωσαν, λυσάντων.
" " Mid. λυέσθωσαν, λυέσθων.
λυσάσθωσαν, λυσάσθων.
" " Pass. λυθήτωσαν, λυθέντων.

Of these forms the longer—those in -σαν—are not found in verse till after Alexander the Great, and are therefore when found in Attic prose texts to be regarded with suspicion.

95. 2nd, 3rd Pers. Sing., 3rd Pers. Pl., 1st Aor. Opt. Active, λύσαις, λύσειας, λύσαι, λύσειε, λύσαιεν, λύσειαν.

Both sets of forms occur, but those formed with ε are the better Attic.

96. Of the Aor. Pass. Opt. λυθείητον, λυθεῖτον, &c., the longer forms are not found in Attic verse.

97. 2nd Pers. Sing. Present and Futures Ind., Mid., and Pass. λύει, λύῃ, &c.

The forms in -ῃ are almost certainly late. The true Attic forms are those in -ει.

98. The better forms for the Pluperf. Act. are as follows—

(1) ἐλελύκη.
(2) ἐλελύκης.
(3) ἐλελύκει, and before a vowel—
ἐλελύκειν.

99. **Auxiliary Tenses.**—The Perfect and Pluperfect Active Indicative may be expressed by the Participle and the substantive Verb, as λελυκώς εἰμι, λελυκὼς ἦν.

The same is true of the Mid. and Pass., as λελυμένος εἰμί, λελυμένος ἦν. The Subj. and Opt. Perf. Act. are more frequently expressed in this way than by λελύκω and λελύκοιμι, namely, λελυκὼς ὦ, λελυκὼς εἴην.

For Future Perfect, λελυκὼς ἔσομαι was used.

100. **The Perfect Imperative.**—This tense is not used in the Active except when the Perfect has a present meaning, and then the 2nd Pers. Sing. always ends in -θι. Thus from κέκρᾱγα, *I shout*, we have the Imperative

(2) κέκραχθι.
(3) κεκραγάτω.
Pl. (2) κεκράγατε.

In the Middle and Passive the 3rd Pers. Singular is common in such phrases as *ταῦτα εἰρήσθω*, *let these things be said.* The 2nd Pers. Sing. is hardly used except when the Perfect has a Present meaning, as, *μέμνησο*, *remember;* from *μέμνημαι*, *I remember; πέπαυσο*, *quiesce.*

101. **Future Middle in Passive Sense.**—In many verbs the Future Middle has a Passive sense. In fact this is so frequently the case that I have placed λύσομαι among the tenses common to Middle and Passive. There are in all about one hundred Verbs which have Futures Middle in form, but Passive in meaning. The larger number of them are from verbs with pure stems, and more than half are from contracted verbs. The following table includes most of those which are found in Attic prose and Comedy.

102. **Contracted Verbs.**

ἀγνοεῖν, be ignorant.
ἀδικεῖν, wrong.
ἀμφισβητεῖν, argue.
ἀνιᾶν, vex.
ἀπατᾶν, deceive.
ἀπιστεῖν, distrust.
ἀφαιρεῖν, take away.
δηλοῦν, show.
ἐᾶν, allow.
ἐλαττοῦσθαι, be worsted.
εὐλογεῖν, praise.
εὐνομεῖσθαι, have good laws.
ζημιοῦν, fine.
ἡττᾶσθαι, be beaten.
θανατοῦν, put to death.
καταφρονεῖν, despise.
κινεῖν, move.
μαρτυρεῖν, bear witness.
μαστιγοῦν, lash.
μισεῖν, hate.
οἰκεῖν, place or *settle.*
ὁμολογεῖν, admit.
παιδαγωγεῖν, educate.
πληροῦν, fill.
πολεμεῖν, make war.
πολιορκεῖν, besiege.
πωλεῖν, sell.
σταθμᾶν, measure.
στερεῖν, bereave.
στρεβλοῦν, rack.
τηρεῖν, observe.
τυραννεῖν, rule.
φθονεῖν, grudge.
φιλεῖν, love.
φρουρεῖν, guard.
ὠφελεῖν, benefit—and others.

103. Verbs from Vowel Stems.

θεραπεύειν, *tend.*
κωλύειν, *hinder.*
-λύειν, *loose.*
παιδεύειν, *educate.*
ἀληθεύειν, *speak truth.*
βουλεύειν, *advise.*
μνημονεύειν, *mention.*
And others.

104. Futures in -ῶ, -οῦμαι.

ἀγωνίζεσθαι, *contend.*
κρίνειν, *decide.*
ὁμαλίζειν, *level.*
ὀργίζειν, *provoke.*
φθείρειν, *destroy.*
And otners.

105. Futures Various.

εἴργειν, *exclude.*
λείπειν, *leave.*
ταράσσειν, *confuse.*
τρέφειν, *nourish.*
φυλάσσειν, *watch.*
ἄγειν, *lead.*
ἄρχειν, *rule.*
And a few others.

106. **Future Middle in Form, Active in Meaning.**—Another peculiarity of the Future is that a very large class of Verbs have a Future Middle in form but Active in meaning. In fact, almost all Verbs which denote the exercise of the bodily functions have this peculiarity. Many of these Verbs are already deponents, and are not included in the following list. The most important are.

107. ᾄδειν, *sing.*
ἀλαλάζειν, *shout.*
βοᾶν, *cry.*
γελᾶν, *laugh.*
γηρύειν, *cry.*
γρύζειν, *grunt.*
κλάζειν, *scream.*
κράζειν, *croak.*
κωκύειν, *wail.*
οἰμώζειν, *lament.*
ὀλολύζειν, *shriek.*
ὀτοτύζειν, *wail.*
ἀκούειν, *hear.*
θιγγάνειν, *touch.*

108. δάκνειν, *bite*. πτύειν, *spit*.
(ἔδειν) ἐσθίειν, *eat*. ῥοφεῖν, *gobble*.
λάπτειν, *lap*. τρώγειν, *gnaw*.
πίνειν, *drink*. χάσκειν, *gape*.

109. ἀπαντᾶν, *meet*. νήχειν, *swim*.
βαδίζειν, *walk*. πηδᾶν, *leap*.
-βαίνειν, *go*. πλεῖν, *sail*.
(βλώσκειν), *go*. ῥεῖν, *flow*.
ἀπο-διδράσκειν, *run away*. σπουδάζειν, *hasten*.
διώκειν, *pursue*. (τρέχειν), *run*,
θεῖν, *run*. φεύγειν, *flee*.
θρώσκειν, *leap*. χωρεῖν, *proceed*.
νεῖν, *swim*. παίζειν, *play*.
πίπτειν, *fall*.
κάμνειν, *be weary*.
φθάνειν, *get before*.
ὑστερεῖν, *be behindhand*.

110. (βιοῦν), *live*. εἶναι, *be*.
-γηράσκειν, *grow old*. θνήσκειν, *die*.
φθινέιν, *decay*. πάσχειν, *suffer*.
(τλᾶν), *endure*.

111. λαγχάνειν, *obtain*. ἁρπάζειν, *seize*.
λαμβάνειν, *take*. κλέπτειν, *steal*.
(κιγχάνειν), *find*. πλεονεκτεῖν, *be grasping*.
τυγχάνειν, *obtain*.

112. Intellectual or Emotional Activity is expressed by

ἁμαρτάνειν, *err*. δείδειν, *fear*.
γιγνώσκειν, *know*. θαυμάζειν, *admire*.
μανθάνειν, *learn*. ἀπολαύειν, enjoy.
σκώπτειν, *jeer*. ὑβρίζειν, insult.
τωθάζειν, *mock*. ὄμνυναι, swear.

113. There are many more, some of which oscillate between the Active and the Middle.

114. **Remarks on Contracted Verbs.**—The following irregularities are to be remembered :—

(1) The Verbs ζῶ, *live ;* χρῶ, *answer* (of an oracle) ; χρῶμαι, *use ;* διψῶ, *thirst ;* πεινῶ, *hunger ;* σμῶ, *smear ;* though from α stems contract in η, as, ζῶ, ζῇς, ζῇ, ζῶμεν, ζῆτε, ζῶσι, Subj., ζῶ, ζῇς, &c., Inf., ζῆν.

κνῶ, *scrape ;* and ψῶ, *rub ;* occasionally contract in η also.

(2) The Verb ῥιγῶ, *shiver with cold,* contracts in ω and ῳ, instead of ου and οι, as, Inf. ῥιγῶν ; Subj. 3 Sing. ῥιγῷ ; Opt. 3 Sing. ῥιγῴη ; Part. ῥιγῶν, ῥιγῶσα, ῥιγῶν, Gen. ῥιγῷντος.

(3) Words like χέω only contract when the vowel ε is followed by another ε and before the endings εις and ει of the Active. In all other cases their formation is identical with that of λύω. The only exception is δέω, *I bind :* which in Attic always contracts like a polysyllable, δῶ, δεῖς, δεῖ, δοῦμεν, δεῖτε, δοῦσι ; Impf. ἔδουν, &c. But δέω, *I lack,* is like all other dissyllabic Verbs in -εω, δέω, δεῖς, δεῖ, δέομεν, δεῖτε, δέουσι ; Impf. ἔδεον, ἔδεις, ἔδει, &c.

(4) The Verb λοέω, *wash,* contracts in Attic to λούω, but those persons which have a short connecting vowel are formed as if from λόω, and then contract ; *e.g.*

λόεμεν	becomes	λοῦμεν.
λόετε	„	λοῦτε.
ἔλοον	„	ἔλουν.
λόεσθαι	„	λοῦσθαι.
λοόμενος	„	λούμενος.

CHAPTER XIII.

THE TENSE-SYSTEM OF REGULAR VERBS IN Ω.

115. You must carefully observe that in no tense of λύω is there any Stem-form shorter than λυ, which we call the Present Stem. It may therefore also be called the Verbal Stem, as there is no part of the Verb in which the syllable λυ is not found. The same is true of all pure Verbs, that is, Verbs which have the ω of the First Person Singular Present Indicative Active preceded by a vowel. Of course contracted Verbs belong to this class, as τιμῶ, φιλῶ, and δηλῶ were originally τιμάω, φιλέω, and δηλόω. This is a very important class of Verbs, and far more Greek Verbs belong to it than to any other.

Many impure Verbs also belong to this group, that is, have their Present Stem and their Verbal Stem identical, such as λέγω, *I say*, and πλέκω, *I plait.* But with most impure Verbs the case is different. Thus of the Verbs which you have learned, if you take φεύγω or λείπω, you will observe that the Present Stems φευγ and λειπ are not the shortest Stem-forms in the Verb. For φεύγω has for Aorist ἔφυγον, of which φυγ is the Stem, and λείπω forms an Aorist ἔλιπον from the Stem λιπ.

116. We may now go further than we did on p. 45, and may divide our Verbs in a better way than by the letters in which their Stems end, for we have learned that some Verbs have no Stem-form shorter than the present Stem and that others have.

This at once separates all Greek Verbs in ω into two *great groups*—

K

I. Verbs in which the Present Stem and Verb-Stem are identical.

II. Verbs in which the Present Stem and Verb-Stem are different.

117. But if we examine the Verbs which belong to the second of these two groups, we shall see that the Present Stem is always derived from the shorter Stem-form or Verb-Stem, but in different ways. We may thus divide the second group into several smaller groups according to the way in which the Verb-Stem is altered to form the Present Stem.

118. I, The *vowel* of the Verb-Stem is lengthened.

φεύγω, *I flee.*	Verb-Stem φυγ.
λείπω, *I leave.*	„ „ λιπ.

119. II. The Consonant τ is attached to the Verb-Stem, generally in cases when the Verb-Stem ends in a Labial.

βλάπτω, *I hurt.*	Verb-Stem, βλαβ.
τίκτω, *I produce.*	„ „ τεκ.

120. III. The vowel ι, or rather the semi-vowel *j* or *y*, is affixed to the Verb-Stem, but produces changes which you must for the present take on trust—

(1) The gutturals κ, γ, χ are by union with it changed to σσ (ττ).

κηρύσσω, *I proclaim*	for	κηρυκ-ι-ω.
ὀρύσσω, *I dig*	for	ὀρυχ-ι-ω.

(2) δ and occasionally γ coalesce with the ι to form ζ.

κομίζω, *I carry*	for	κομιδ-ι-ω.
κράζω, *I cry*	for	κραγ-ι-ω.

(3) λ by union with the ι becomes λλ.

βάλλω, *I throw*	for	βαλ-ι-ω.
στέλλω, *I equip*	for	στελ-ι-ω.

(4) When the Verb-Stem ends in ν or ρ the ι is thrown back into it.

τείνω, *I stretch* for τεν-ι-ω.
φθείρω, *I destroy* for φθερ-ι-ω.

121. IV. The Verb-Stem is lengthened by ν or a syllable containing ν.

(1) ν alone is added, the Stem-vowel being also often lengthened.

βαίνω, *I go.* Verb-Stem βᾰ.
ἐλαύνω, *I drive.* „ „ ἐλᾰ
τέμνω, *I cut.* „ „ τεμ.

(2) The syllable αν is added.

βλαστάνω, *I grow.* Verb-Stem βλαστ.

(3) The syllable νε is added.

κυνέω, *I kiss.* Verb-Stem κυ.

122. V. The Verb-Stem is enlarged by σκ, which is added to Vowel-stems directly, but to Consonant-stems after inserting ι. A few Verbs are also reduplicated. The σκ like *sc* in Latin had originally an inchoative sense.

γηράσκω, *I grow old.* Verb-Stem γηρᾱ.
γιγνώσκω, *I recognise* [*(g)nosco*]. „ „ γνω.

The last two classes must be regarded as quite irregular.

Still more irregular are the two remaining classes.

123. VI. A short Stem alternates with one enlarged by ε.

(1) The enlarged Stem in ε belongs to the Present, while the other tenses are formed from the shorter.

δοκῶ (έω), *I seem.* Verb-Stem δοκ.
Fut. δόξω (not δοκήσω).

(2) The shorter Stem belongs to the Present, while the other tenses are formed from the enlarged Stem.

θέλω, *I wish.*	Verb-Stem θελε.
	Fut. θελήσω (not θελῶ).

124. VII. The Verb draws upon quite different Stems to form its different tenses, as ὁρῶ, *I see;* ὄψομαι, *I shall see;* εἶδον, *I saw*, from ὁρα, ὀπ, ἰδ.

CHAPTER XIV.

THE TENSES IN DETAIL.

125. **Present and Imperfect.**—The Imperfect is formed from the Present Stem by prefixing the augment and adding the personal endings.

Verbs when compounded with a Preposition have the augment immediately after a Preposition, as εἰσβάλλω, *I throw into*, εἰσ-έ-βαλλον; εἰσάγω, *I introduce*, εἰσ-ῆγον. The Prepositions σύν, *with*, and ἐν, *in*, which become assimilated to the first consonant of the simple Verb, resume their true forms before the augment, συμβάλλω, *I throw together*, συν-έ-βαλλον, ἐμβάλλω, *I throw into*, ἐν-έ-βαλλον. ἐκ, *out of*, becomes ἐξ.

126. When the Preposition ends in a vowel, the vowel is elided before the augment, ὑπο-γράφω, *I subscribe*, ὑπ-έ-γραφον. But περί, *about*, and πρό, *before*, never lose their vowel, although πρό may contract with ε to form ου, as προὔβαινον for προ-έ-βαινον, *I went forward*. There are some irregularities in augment.

127. (1) ε becomes ει, not η, in the Verbs—

ἐᾶν, *leave.*	ἕπεσθαι, *follow.*
ἐθίζειν, *become used.*	ἔχειν, *have.*
ἑστιᾶν, *entertain.*	ἑλίσσειν, *roll.*
ἕλκειν, *draw.*	ἕρπειν, *creep.*

128. (2) Some Verbs beginning with a vowel have the temporal augment—

ὠνεῖσθαι, *buy.*	ἐωνούμην.
ὠθεῖν, *push.*	ἐώθουν.
οὐρεῖν, *make water.*	ἐούρουν.

129. (3) Some Verbs have a double augment in Attic—

ἀντιβολεῖν, *entreat.*	ἠντεβόλουν.
ἀντιδικεῖν, *dispute.*	ἠντεδίκουν.
ἀμφισβητεῖν, *dissent.*	ἠμφεσβήτουν.
ἀμφιγνοεῖν, *doubt.*	ἠμφέγνουν.
διαιτᾶν, *diet.*	ἐδιῄτων.
διακονεῖν, *serve.*	ἐδιηκόνουν.
ἀνέχεσθαι, *endure.*	ἠνειχόμην.
ἐνοχλεῖν, *trouble.*	ἠνώχλουν.
ἀνοιγνύναι, *open.*	ἀνέῳγον.
ἀμπέχεσθαι, *have on.*	ἠμπειχόμην.

130. **The Second or Strong Aorist Active and Middle.**—Pure Verbs cannot form this tense, and few even of impure Verbs possess it. It is consequently very rare in Greek, hardly occurring at all except in such Verbs as have a root for their Stem. Its inflexion is for the Indicative the same as that of the Imperfect, and for the other moods the same as that of the Present. Thus from λείπω we have the Active Aorist ἔλιπον, and from πείθω the Middle Aorist ἐπιθόμην.

Active.

Imperfect. / Present.

	Imperfect. *Indicative.*		Present. *Subjunctive.*	*Optative.*
S. 1.	ἔλειπον.	*Was, were leaving.*	λείπω.	λείποιμι.
2.	ἔλειπες.			
3.	ἔλειπε.		*Imperative.*	*Infinitive.*
D. 2.	ἐλείπετον.		λεῖπε.	λείπειν.
3.	ἐλειπέτην.			
P. 1.	ἐλείπομεν.			
2.	ἐλείπετε.		*Participle.*	
3.	ἔλειπον.		λείπων, λείπουσα, λεῖπον.	

Aorist.

S. 1.	ἔλιπον.	*Left.*	λίπω	λίποιμι.
2.	ἔλιπες.			
3.	ἔλιπε.			
D. 2.	ἐλίπετον.		λίπε.	λιπεῖν,
3.	ἐλιπέτην.			
P. 1.	ἐλίπομεν.			
2.	ἐλίπετε.			
3.	ἔλιπον.		λιπών, λιποῦσα, λιπόν.	

Middle.

	Imperfect. *Indicative.*		Present. *Subjunctive.*	*Optative.*
S. 1.	ἐπειθόμην.	*Was, were believing.*	πείθωμαι.	πειθοίμην.
2.	ἐπείθου.			
3.	ἐπείθετο.		*Imperative.*	*Infinitive.*
D. 2.	ἐπείθεσθον.		πείθου.	πείθεσθαι.
3.	ἐπειθέσθην.			
P. 1.	ἐπειθόμεθα.			
2.	ἐπείθεσθε.		*Participle.*	
3.	ἐπείθοντο.		πειθόμενος, η, ον.	

AORIST.

		Believed.		
S.	1. ἐπιθόμην.		*Subjunctive.*	*Optative.*
	2. ἐπίθου.		πίθωμαι.	πιθοίμην.
	3. ἐπίθετο.			
D.	2. ἐπίθεσθον.		*Imperative.*	*Infinitive.*
	3. ἐπιθέσθην.		πίθου.	πιθέσθαι.
P.	1. ἐπιθόμεθα.			
	2. ἐπίθεσθε.		*Participle.*	
	3. ἐπίθοντο.		πιθόμενος, η, ον.	

131. **Future Active and Middle.**—The inflexion of the Future is the same as that of the Present, except that the Future Stem forms no Subjunctive or Imperative. The contracted Future has the same inflexion as contracted Presents. *E.g.*—

	PRESENT.	FUTURE.
	Indicative.	
S.	1. φιλῶ, *I love.*	σπερῶ, *I shall sow.*
	2. φιλεῖς.	σπερεῖς.
	3. φιλεῖ.	σπερεῖ.
D.	2. φιλεῖτον.	σπερεῖτον.
	3. φιλεῖτον.	σπερεῖτον.
P.	1. φιλοῦμεν.	σπεροῦμεν.
	2. φιλεῖτε.	σπερεῖτε.
	3. φιλοῦσι.	σπεροῦσι.
	Optative.	
S.	1. φιλοίην.	σπεροίην.
	2. φιλοίης.	σπεροίης.
	3. φιλοίη.	σπεροίη.
D.	2. φιλοῖτον, &c.	σπεροῖτον, &c.
	Infinitive.	
	φιλεῖν.	σπερεῖν.
	Participle.	
	φιλῶν, -ουσα, -οῦν.	σπερῶν, -οῦσα, -οῦν.

And so with the Middle.

132. All Stems ending in a vowel or a mute form their Future by adding σ to the Stem. The σ combines with gutturals to form ξ, and with labials to form ψ, while dentals are dropped before it. πλέκ-ω, *I plait*, πλέξω; βλάπ-τω, *I hurt*, βλάψω; ᾄδ-ω, *I sing*, ᾄσομαι; πράσσω, *do* (πραγ), πράξω.

Vowel Stems have their vowels long before σ, that is, ε becomes η, ο becomes ω, ᾰ if preceded by ε, ι, or ρ becomes α, in all other cases η; as ποιῶ (έω), ποιήσω; δηλῶ (όω), δηλώσω; ἐῶ (άω), *allow*, ἐάσω; ἰῶμαι (ἰάομαι), *heal*, ἰάσομαι; φυρῶ (άω), *knead*, φυράσω; but βοῶ (άω), *shout*; βοήσομαι; τιμῶ (άω), τιμήσω.

133. The contracted Future is formed by adding εω to the Verb-Stem, and then contracting; as τεν (Verb-Stem of τείνω, *stretch*), Fut. τενέω, τενῶ. Stems ending in λ, μ, ν, ρ form their Futures in this way. The syllable preceding the contracted syllable is always short, νέμω, *assign*, νεμῶ; μιαίνω, *pollute*, μιανῶ; σπείρω, *sow*, σπερῶ; ἀγγέλλω, *report*, ἀγγελῶ.

134. Not a few Stems in ε (Pres. έω), most Stems in ιδ (Pres. ίζω), and a very few in αδ (Pres. άζω), throw out the σ in the Future. Those in ε and αδ at once contract the colliding vowels, καλῶ (έω), *call*; Fut. καλῶ (for καλέσω); βιβάζω, *bring*; Fut. βιβῶ (for βιβάσω). But the Stems in ιδ after dropping σ add ε and contract, as πορίζω, *provide*,ποριῶ for (ποριέω).

135. **The First or Weak Aorist Active and Middle.**—The Stem is simply the Future Stem lengthened by α.

The Stems in λ, μ, ν, ρ which form their Future without σ do not employ that letter in the Aorist, but in compensation lengthen their vowel; ᾰ after ι and ρ becomes ᾱ, after other vowels and after consonants η, ῥαίνω, *sprinkle*, ἔρρᾱνα; καθαίρω, *purify*, ἐκάθηρα.

Exceptions are—

μιαίνω, *pollute*, ἐμίηνα.
τετραίνω, *bore*, ἐτέτρηνα.

κοιλαίνω, *hollow*, ἐκοίλᾱνα.
λευκαίνω, *whiten*, ἐλύκᾱνα.
ὀργαίνω, *enrage*, ὤργᾱνα.
ἰσχναίνω, *dry*, ἴσχνανα.

ε becomes ει, and ι and υ are simply lengthened, as μένω, *remain*, ἔμεινα; κρίνω, *decide*, ἔκρῑνα.

136. **The Perfect Active.**—The same Stem also supplies the Pluperfect Active, the Perfect and Pluperfect Middle and Passive, and the Third Future, which has a Passive sense.

The characteristic mark of the Stem is its reduplication. The rules for reduplication are—

137. (1) Verbs beginning with a vowel have no reduplication proper, but simply lengthen the vowel, as ὁρμῶ (άω), *urge*, ὥρμηκα.

138. (2) Verbs beginning with a consonant followed by a vowel or by λ, ν, or ρ, repeat the initial consonant with ε, as λύω, λέλῠκα—γράφω, *write*, γέγρᾰφα; πλέκω, *plait*, πέπλεχα; κνάω, *scrape*, κέκναικα. But an aspirate is represented by the corresponding tenuis, as φιλῶ, πεφίληκα.

139. (3) In all other cases a Verb beginning with two consonants takes only ε for its reduplication, as κτείνω, *kill*, ἔκτονα; ζημιῶ, *injure*, ἐζημίωκα.

Exceptions to (2) are all Verbs beginning with ρ, γλ, γν, μν, which follow (3), as, ῥίπτω, *throw*, ἔρρῑφα; γλύφω, *carve*, ἔγλυμμαι (Pass.); μνημονεύω, *mention*, ἐμνημόνευκα; βλαστάνω, *grow*, ἐβλάστηκα.

140. There is a strong and a weak Perfect Active.

The Weak Perfect Active.—κ is added to the *reduplicated* Verb-Stem, the vowel following the rules laid down *in § 132.*

δρῶ (άω), *do*, δράσω, δέδρακα.
τιμῶ (άω), τιμήσω, τετίμηκα.

141. Stems in τ, δ, θ, throw out these consonants before κ, as ὀνειδίζω (ὀνειδ), *reproach*, ὠνείδικα; πείθω (πιθ), *persuade*, πέπεικα. The vowel is occasionally changed, as φθείρω (φθερ), *destroy*, ἔφθαρκα.

142. **The Second or Strong Perfect.**—This is an old and comparatively rare form, formed directly from the Verb-Stem. The vowel of the Stem undergoes change, and a few Stems in κ, γ, π, β, change these letters into the corresponding aspirates, as φεύγω (φυγ) *flee*, πέφευγα; πέμπω (πεμπ), *send*, πέπομφα.

143. **The Perfect Middle and Passive.**—This tense is formed by adding the personal endings of the principal tenses of the Middle directly to the Perfect-Stem without any connecting vowel. Stem λυ, Perfect-Stem λελυ, Perf. Mid. λέλυ-μαι. When the Stem ends in a consonant, the consonant is changed according to the rules laid down in page 73. The ending -νται of the Third Person Plural is incompatible with Consonantal Stems, and in this case the periphrasis with εἰμί is always used. The following table gives an example of each class of Consonant Stems—

GUTTURAL.	LABIAL.	DENTAL.	LIQUID, &c.
	Singular.		
πέπλεγμαι.	γέγραμμαι.	πέπεισμαι.	ἔσπαρμαι.
πέπλεξαι.	γέγραψαι.	πέπεισαι.	ἔσπαρσαι.
πέπλεκται.	γέγραπται.	πέπεισται.	ἔσπαρται.
	Plural.		
πεπλέγμεθα.	γεγράμμεθα.	πεπείσμεθα.	ἐσπάρμεθα.
πέπλεχθε.	γέγραφθε.	πέπεισθε.	ἔσπαρθε.
πεπλεγμένοι εἰσι.	γεγραμμένοι εἰσι.	πεπεισμένοι εἰσι.	ἐσπαρμένοι εἰσι.

144. **The Future Perfect** is formed by enlarging the Perfect Stem by σ and adding the inflexions of the

Future Middle, as *λελυ-σ-ομαι*, from *λελυ*; *λελείψομαι*, from *λελειπ*.

145. **The Second or Strong Aorist Passive Stem.**—This Stem supplies the Second Aorist and the Second Future Passive. It is formed by adding *ε* to the Verb-Stem, the Stem-vowel being sometimes changed, as *τήκω*, *melt* (Verb-Stem *τᾰκ*); *ἐτάκην* (Stem *τᾰκε*); *πλέκω*, *plait* (Verb-Stem *πλεκ*); *ἐπλάκην* (Stem *πλακε*).

146. **The First or Weak Aorist Passive Stem.**—This Stem supplies the First Aorist and the First Future Passive, and is formed from the Verbal Stem by adding *θε*. Before this syllable the vowel of Vowel Stems is lengthened as in the Future, Aorist, and Perfect Active, *τιμα*, *ἐτιμήθην*; *πειρα*, *try*, *ἐπειράθην*; Futures, *τιμηθήσομαι*, *πειραθήσομαι*.

CHAPTER XV.

VERBS IN -*μι*.

147. THESE Verbs differ from the Verbs in *ω* only in the inflexion of the Present and Second Aorist Stems, and occasionally in that of the Perfect and Pluperfect. Many Verbs belonging to the -*ω* Conjugation form their Aorist Active according to the -*μι* Conjugation.

148. They are divided into two classes.

(1) Verbs which in the Present add their person-endings directly to the Verb-Stem or the Verb-Stem reduplicated with *ι*; as, *φή-μι*, *I say*; *τί-θη-μι*, *I place*.

(2) Verbs which add *νυ* to the Verb-Stem in order to form the Present Stem; as, *δείκ-νῡ-μι*, *I show* (Verb-Stem *δεικ*).

We shall add a few more Verbs conjugated in full to those already given. The rest you will find in the list of Verbs on p. 131.

149. ἵημι, *I send, make to go;* is inflected like τίθημι.

Active.

Pres. ἵημι, ἵης, ἵησι (ν), ἵεμεν, ἵετε, ἱᾶσι (ν).

Subj. ἱῶ; Opt. ἱείην; Imper. ἵει; Inf. ἱέναι; Part. ἱείς.

Imperf. ἵην, ἵεις, ἵει, ἵεμεν, ἵετε, ἵεσαν.

Aor. ἧκα, ἧκας, ἧκε (ν), εἷμεν, εἷτε, εἷσαν or ἧκαν.

Subj. ὧ; Opt. εἵην; Imper. ἕς; Inf. εἷναι; Part. εἵς.

Fut. ἥσω; Perf. εἷκα.

Middle.

ἵεμαι, *I hasten;* Subj. ἱῶμαι, ἱῇ, ἱῆται, &c.

Opt. ἱείμην or ἱοίμην; Imper. ἵεσο; Inf. ἵεσθαι; Part. ἱέμενος.

Imperf. ἱέμην, ἵεσο.

Aorist εἵμην, εἷσο, εἷτο, &c.; Subj. ὧμαι.

Opt. εἵμην or οἵμην.

Fut. ἥσομαι; Perf. εἷμαι; Plupf. εἵμην.

Aor. Pass. εἵθην; Subj. ἑθῶ; Fut. ἑθήσομαι.

Verbals ἑτός, ἑτέος.

It differs from τίθημι in the 2nd form of the Optative Middle, and its Perfect Middle has, unlike τέθειμαι, a Passive as well as a Middle sense.

150. The three Aorists ἔθηκα, ἧκα, and ἔδωκα are (with the rare ἔφρηκα) the only Greek Aorists in -κα.

151. φημί, *I say;* φής, φησί, φαμέν, φατέ, φασί.

Subj. φῶ; Opt. φαίην; Imper. φάθί or φάθι.

Inf. φάναι; Part. φάς.

Imperf. ἔφην, ἔφησθα, ἔφη, ἔφάμεν, ἔφάτε, ἔφάσαν.

152. Besides the regular forms the Perfect Act. of ἵστημι has also the following—

P. 1. ἕστᾰμεν, *we stand.*
2. ἕστᾰτε.
3. ἑστᾶσι. Pluperf. ἕστᾰσαν, *they stood.*

Subj. ἑστῶ, *I may stand;* ἑστῶμεν, ἑστῶσι; Opt. ἑσταίην; Imper. ἕστᾰθι, ἑστάτω, ἕστᾰτον, ἕστᾰτε; Inf. ἑστᾱ́ναι; Part. ἑστώς, ἑστῶσα, ἑστός; Gen. ἑστῶτος, ἑστώσης.

153. Similarly τέθνηκα, the Perf. of θνήσκω, *I die;* has the forms τέθνᾰμεν, τέθνᾰτε, τεθνᾶσι, 3 Pl. Plupf. ἐτέθνασαν; Imper. τέθναθι, τεθνᾱ́τω; Inf. τεθνᾱ́ναι; Part. τεθνεώς, τεθνεῶσα, τεθνεός.

154. δέδῐα or δέδοικα (Stem δι), *I fear.*

PERFECT.	PLUPERFECT.
(δέδοικα) δέδια.	ἐδεδοίκη.
δέδοικας.	ἐδεδοίκης.
δέδοικε (δέδιε).	ἐδεδοίκει (ν) (ἐδεδίει).
(δεδοίκαμεν) δέδιμεν.	ἐδέδιμεν.
δεδοίκατε, δέδιτε.	ἐδέδιτε.
δεδίασι (ν).	ἐδέδισαν.

Subj. δεδίω.
Imper. δέδῐθι, δεδίτω, δέδιτε.
Inf. δεδιέναι (δεδοικέναι).
Part. δεδιώς, δεδιυῖα, δεδιός.
(δεδοικώς, δεδοικυῖα, δεδοικός.)

155. The following Verbs are from Consonant-Stems.

οἶδα, *I know.*

	INDICATIVE.	SUBJUNCTIVE.	OPTATIVE.
	Present.		
S.	1. οἶδα.	εἰδῶ.	εἰδείην.
	2. οἶσθα.	εἰδῇς.	εἰδείης.
	3. οἶδε (ν).	εἰδῇ.	εἰδείη.

	INDICATIVE.	SUBJUNCTIVE.	OPTATIVE.
	Present.		
D.	2. ἴστον.	εἰδῆτον.	εἰδεῖτον.
	3. ἴστον.	εἰδῆτον.	εἰδείτην.
P.	1. ἴσμεν.	εἰδῶμεν.	εἰδεῖμεν.
	2. ἴστε.	εἰδῆτε.	εἰδεῖτε.
	3. ἴσασι (ν).	εἰδῶσι (ν).	εἰδεῖεν.

	Past.	IMPERATIVE.	INFINITIVE.
S.	1. ᾔδη.		εἰδέναι.
	2. ᾔδησθα.	ἴσθι.	
	3. ᾔδει (ν).	ἴστω.	PARTICIPLE.
D.	2. ᾖστον.	ἴστον.	εἰδώς, εἰδυῖα, εἰδός.
	3. ᾔστην.	ἴστων.	VERBAL.
P.	1. ᾖσμεν.		ἰστέον.
	2. ᾖστε.	ἴστε.	
	3. ᾖσαν.	ἴστων or ἴστωσαν.	
	Future.		
	εἴσομαι.		
	Regular.		

156. The forms οἴδαμεν, οἴδατε, οἴδασι for the Plural of the Present are still found occasionally in some texts of Attic writers, but ought undoubtedly to be removed. The same is the case with the Past forms given below.

They are dialectical and late.

S. 1. ᾔδειν.
 2. ᾔδεισθα, ᾔδεις or ᾔδης.
 3. ᾔδη.
D. 2. ᾔδειτον.
 3. ᾐδείτην.
P. 1. ᾔδειμεν.
 2. ᾔδειτε.

157. ἔοικα, *I am like.*

	INDICATIVE.	SUBJUNCTIVE.	OPTATIVE.
	Present.		
S.	1. ἔοικα.	ἐοίκω.	ἐοίκοιμι.
	2. ἔοικας.	*Regular, or*	*Regular, or*
	3. ἔοικε (ν).	εἰκὼς ὦ, ᾖς, &c.	εἰκὼς εἴην, &c.
D.	2. ἐοίκατον.		
	3. ἐοίκατον.	*Infinitive.*	*Part.*
P.	1. ἔοιγμεν.	εἰκέναι.	εἰκώς, εἰκυῖα, εἰκός.
	2. ἐοίκατε.		
	3. εἴξασι (ν).		
	Past.		
	3. Sing. ᾔκει (ν).		
	3. Pl. ἐῴκεσαν.		
	Future.		
	εἴξω, *regular.*		

The forms ἐοίκαμεν for ἔοιγμεν and ἐοίκασι (ν) for εἴξασι (ν) as well as ἐοικέναι and ἐοικώς, for εἰκέναι and εἰκώς, are probably un-Attic.

CHAPTER XVI.

THE following list contains only the most commonly occurring of irregular and defective Attic Verbs.

ᾄδω, *sing.* F. ᾄσομαι. A. ᾖσα. Pass. A. ᾔσθην. Perf. ᾖσμαι.

αἰνῶ, *praise;* αἰνέσω, ᾔνεσα, ᾔνεκα, ᾔνημαι, ᾐνέθην.

αἰσθάνομαι, *perceive;* αἰσθήσομαι, ᾔσθημαι, ᾐσθόμην.

ἀκούω, *hear;* ἀκούσομαι, ἤκουσα, ἀκήκοα, ἠκούσθην, ἀκουσθήσομαι.

ἁμαρτάνω, *err* ; ἁμαρτήσομαι, ἡμάρτηκα, ἥμαρτον, ἡμάρτημαι, ἡμαρτήθην.

ἀναλίσκω, *expend* ; ἀναλώσω, ἀνάλωσα or ἀνήλωσα, ἀνάλωκα or ἀνήλωκα, ἀνάλωμαι or ἀνήλωμαι, ἀναλώθην or ἀνηλώθην.

ἀνοίγνυμι, *open* ; Imp. ἀνέῳγον, ἀνοίξω, ἀνέῳξα, ἀνέῳχα, ἀνέῳγμαι, ἀνεῴχθην.

ἅπτομαι, *touch* ; ἅψομαι, ἡψάμην, ἧμμαι (*have touched*).

ἅπτω, *kindle* ; ἅψω, ἧψα, ἧμμαι, ἥφθην.

ἁρπάζω, *seize* ; ἁρπάσομαι, ἥρπασα, ἥρπακα, ἥρπασμαι, ἡρπάσθην.

ἄρχομαι, *begin* ; ἄρξομαι, ἠρξάμην, ἦργμαι (*have begun*).

ἄρχω, *rule* ; ἄρξω, ἦρξα, ἤρχθην, ἄρξομαι (*shall be ruled*).

αὐξάνω, *make to grow* ; αὐξήσω, ηὔξησα, ηὔξηκα, Mid. and Pass., *to grow, be increased*, αὐξήσομαι, ηὔξημαι, ηὐξήθην.

ἀφικνοῦμαι, *come* ; ἀφίξομαι, ἀφικόμην, ἀφῖγμαι.

βαίνω, *go* ; -βήσομαι, βέβηκα, Aor. ἔβην, Imper. βῆθι, (-βά), βῆναι, βάς, -βέβἄμαι, -ἐβάθην.

βάλλω, *throw* ; βαλῶ, βέβληκα, ἔβἄλον, βέβλημαι, ἐβλήθην, βληθήσομαι.

βλάπτω, *hurt* ; βλάψω, ἔβλαψα, βέβλαφα, βέβλαμμαι, ἐβλάφθην, ἐβλάβην, βλαβήσομαι.

βλέπω, *see* ; βλέψομαι, ἔβλεψα.

(βλώσκω), *go* ; μολοῦμαι, ἔμολον, μέμβλωκα.

βούλομαι, *wish* ; βουλήσομαι, βεβούλημαι (*have wished*), ἐβουλήθην (*I wished*).

βοῶ (άω), *shout* ; βοήσομαι, ἐβόησα.

γαμῶ, *marry, duco uxorem* ; γαμῶ, ἔγημα, γεγάμηκα, Mid. γαμοῦμαι, *nubo* ; γαμοῦμαι, ἐγημάμην, γεγάμημαι.

γελῶ (άω), *laugh* ; γελάσομαι, Aor. Pass. ἐγελάσθην.

γηράσκω, *grow old* ; γηράσομαι.

γίγνομαι, *become* ; γενήσομαι, ἐγενόμην, γεγένημαι, γέγονα, *am*.

γιγνώσκω, *recognise* ; γνώσομαι, ἔγνωκα (intellexi), ἔγνωσμαι, ἐγνώσθην; 2 Aor. Act. ἔγνων, *I perceived*; Subj. γνῶ, γνῷς, &c.; Opt. γνοίην; Imper. γνῶθι; Inf. γνῶναι; Part. γνούς.

δάκνω, *bite*; δήξομαι, ἔδακον, δέδηγμαι, ἐδήχθην.

δείκνυμι, *show*; δείξω, ἔδειξα, δέδειχα, δείξομαι, ἐδειξάμην, δέδειγμαι, ἐδείχθην, δειχθήσομαι.

δέχομαι, *receive*; δέξομαι, ἐδεξάμην, δέδεγμαι, ἐδέχθην.

δέω, *bind*; δήσω, ἔδησα, δέδεκα, δέδεμαι, ἐδέθην, δεθήσομαι, δεδήσομαι, see p. 116, § 114 (3).

δέω, *lack*; δεήσω, δεδέηκα; Mid. *want*, *beseech*, δεήσομαι, δεδέημαι, ἐδεήθην (*I besought*).

διδάσκω, *teach*; διδάξω, δεδίδαχα, διδάξομαι, ἐδιδαξάμην, δεδίδαγμαι, ἐδιδάχθην.

δύναμαι, *be able*; δυνήσομαι, δεδύνημαι, ἐδυνήθην.

ἐγείρω, *arouse*; ἐγερῶ, ἤγειρα, ἐγήγερμαι, ἠγέρθην, ἐγερθήσομαι, ἐγρήγορα, *I am awake*.

ἐθέλω, *wish*; ἐθελήσω, ἠθέληκα, ἠθέλησα.

ἐθίζω, *accustom*; ἐθιῶ, εἴθισα, εἴθικα, εἴθισμαι.

ἐλαύνω, *drive*, *march*; Fut. ἐλῶ, ἤλασα, ἐλήλακα, ἐλήλαμαι, ἠλάθην.

ἕλκω, *draw*; ἕλξω, εἵλκυσα, εἵλκυκα, εἵλκυσμαι.

ἐπίσταμαι, *know*; ἠπιστάμην, ἐπιστήσομαι, ἠπιστήθην.

ἕπομαι, *follow*; εἱπόμην, ἕψομαι, ἑσπόμην and -ἑσπόμην, Subj. σπῶμαι, &c.

ἐργάζομαι, *work*; ἐργάσομαι, εἰργασάμην, εἴργασμαι (*have done or been done*), εἰργάσθην.

εὑρίσκω, *find*; εὑρήσω, ηὗρον, ηὕρηκα, ηὑρόμην, ηὕρημαι, ηὑρέθην, εὑρεθήσομαι.

ἔχω, *have*; εἶχον, ἕξω or σχήσω, ἔσχηκα, 2 Aor. ἔσχον, σχῶ, σχοίην (-σχοῖμι), σχεῖν, σχών.

ἐῶ (άω), *permit*; ἐάσω, εἴᾱσα, εἴᾱκα, εἴᾱμαι, εἰάθην, ἐάσομαι as Pass.

ζεύγνυμι, *yoke*; ζεύξω, ἔζευξα, ἔζευγμαι, ἐζύγην.

ἥδομαι, *am glad*; ἡσθήσομαι, ἥσθην.

θάπτω, *bury;* θάψω, ἔθαψα, τέθαμμαι, ἐτάφην, ταφήσομαι, τεθάψομαι.

καθαίρω, *purify;* καθαρῶ, ἐκάθηρα, κεκάθαρμαι, ἐκαθάρθην.

καθέζομαι, *sit down;* καθεδοῦμαι, ἐκαθεζόμην as Impf. and Aorist.

κάθημαι, *sit;* ἐκαθήμην or καθήμην.

καλῶ, (έω), *call;* καλῶ, ἐκάλεσα, κέκληκα, κέκλημαι, ἐκλήθην, κληθήσομαι, κεκλήσομαι.

κάμνω, *labour;* καμοῦμαι, ἔκαμον, κέκμηκα.

κάω, *burn;* (also καίω), καύσω (or -ομαι), ἔκαυσα, κέκαυκα, κέκαυμαι, ἐκαύθην.

κεῖμαι, *lie, have been placed;* used as the Passive Perfect of τίθημι, τέθειμαι, having only a Middle sense.

κεράννυμι, *mix;* ἐκέρασα, κέκρāμαι.

κερδαίνω, *gain;* κερδανῶ, ἐκέρδāνα.

κλάω, *weep;* κλαύσομαι (or κλαήσω), ἔκλαυσα.

κλέπτω, *steal;* κλέψω (or κλέψομαι), ἔκλεψα, κέκλοφα, κέκλεμμαι, ἐκλάπην.

κρεμάννυμι, *hang;* κρεμῶ (άσω), ἐκρέμασα, ἐκρεμάσθην.

κρίνω, *judge;* κρινῶ, ἔκρῑνα, κέκρῐκα, κέκρῐμαι, ἐκρίθην, κριθήσομαι.

κτῶμαι (αο), *acquire;* κτήσομαι, ἐκτησάμην, κέκτημαι (*I possess*); Subj. κεκτῶμαι; Opt. κεκτῄμην; κεκτήσομαι, *shall possess;* ἐκτήθην, *was obtained.*

λαγχάνω, *obtain by lot;* λήξομαι, ἔλαχον, εἴληχα, εἴληγμαι, εἰλήχθην.

λαμβάνω, *receive;* λήψομαι, ἔλαβον, εἴληφα, εἴλημμαι, ἐλήφθην, ληφθήσομαι.

λανθάνω, *lie hid;* λήσω, ἔλαθον, λέληθα; Mid. *forget,* λήσομαι, ἐλαθόμην, λέλησμαι.

λουώ, *wash;* see p. 116, § 114 (4).

μανθάνω, *learn;* μαθήσομαι, ἔμαθον, μεμάθηκα.

μάχομαι, *fight;* Fut. μαχοῦμαι, ἐμαχεσάμην, μεμάχημαι.

μίγνυμι, *mix;* μίξω, ἔμιξα, μέμιγμαι, ἐμίχθην, ἐμίγην.

μιμνήσκομαι, *remember, mention;* Perf. μέμνημαι, *I remember*, μεμνήσομαι, ἐμνήσθην, *I remembered*, μνησθήσομαι. Like κέκτημαι and κέκλημαι, μέμνημαι forms its Subj. and Opt. singularly, μεμνῶμαι, μεμνῄμην; μέμνησο, *remember thou.*

νέμω, *distribute;* νεμῶ, ἔνειμα, νενέμηκα, νενέμημαι, ἐνεμήθην.

νίζω, *wash (hands)*; νίψω, ἔνιψα, νένιμμαι.

νομίζω, *think;* νομιῶ, ἐνόμισα, νενόμικα, νενόμισμαι, ἐνομίσθην.

οἴομαι, *think;* οἰήσομαι, ᾠήθην, but 1st Sing. Pres. Ind. is contracted to οἶμαι, and the Impf. to ᾤμην.

οἴχομαι, *be gone*, οἰχήσομαι.

ὄλλυμι, *destroy, lose;* ὀλῶ, ὤλεσα, -ολώλεκα, 2nd Perf. ὄλωλα, *I perish;* Mid. ὄλλυμαι, *perish;* ὀλοῦμαι, ὠλόμην, generally compounded with ἀπό.

ὄμνυμι, *swear;* ὀμοῦμαι, ὤμοσα, ὀμώμοκα, ὀμώμομαι, ὠμόθην.

ὀσφραίνομαι, *smell;* ὀσφρήσομαι, ὠσφρόμην.

ὀφείλω, *owe;* ὀφειλήσω, ὠφείλησα, ὤφελον, *used in wishes (I ought to), Oh that!*

ὀφλισκάνω, *be guilty, incur (disgrace, &c.)*; ὀφλήσω, ὦφλον, ὤφληκα, ὤφλημαι.

παίζω, *play;* παιξοῦμαι, ἔπαισα, πέπαικα, πέπαισμαι.

πάσχω, *suffer;* πείσομαι, ἔπαθον, πέπονθα.

πετάννυμι, *expand;* πετῶ (άσω), ἐπέτασα, πέπταμαι, ἐπετάσθην.

πήγνυμι, *fasten;* πήξω, ἔπηξα, 2nd Aor. Pass. ἐπάγην, παγήσομαι; 2nd Perf. πέπηγα, *am fixed.*

πίμπλημι, *fill;* πλήσω, ἔπλησα, πέπληκα, πέπλησμαι, ἐπλήσθην.

πίμπρημι, *burn;* πρήσω, ἔπρησα, πέπρημαι, ἐπρήσθην.

πίνω, *drink;* F. πίομαι, ἔπιον, πέπωκα, πέπομαι, ἐπόθην.

πίπτω, *fall;* πεσοῦμαι, ἔπεσον, πέπτωκα.

πλέω, *sail;* πλεύσομαι or πλευσοῦμαι, ἔπλευσα, πέπλευκα, πέπλευσμαι.

πράσσω, *do, fare;* πράξω, ἔπραξα, πέπρᾱχα, πέπραγμαι, ἐπράχθην, &c.; 2nd Perf. πέπρᾱγα, *have fared.*

πυνθᾰνομαι, *hear, enquire;* πεύσομαι, πέπυσμαι, ἐπυθόμην.

ῥέω, *flow;* ῥεύσομαι, ἔρρευσα, ἐρρύηκα, ἐρρύην, ῥυήσομαι.

ῥήγνυμι, *break;* ῥήξω, ἔρρηξα, ἐρρᾰγην, ῥαγήσομαι; 2nd Perf. ἔρρωγα, *am broken.*

ῥίπτω, *throw;* ῥίψω, ἔρριψα, ἔρρῑφα, ἔρριμμαι, ἐρρίφθην.

σβέννυμι, *quench;* σβέσω, ἔσβεσα, ἔσβην, *I was quenched;* ἔσβηκα, *am quenched.*

σκώπτω, *jeer;* σκώψομαι, ἐσκώφθην.

στέλλω, *despatch;* στελῶ, ἔστειλα, ἔσταλκα, ἔσταλμαι, ἐστάλην.

στρέφω, *turn;* στρέψω, ἔστρεψα, ἔστραμμαι, ἐστράφην.

τείνω, *stretch;* τενῶ, ἔτεινα, τέτᾰκα, τέτᾰμαι, ἐτᾰθην.

τέμνω, *cut;* τεμῶ, ἔτεμον, τέτμηκα, τέτμημαι, ἐτμήθην; Mid. τεμοῦμαι, ἐτεμόμην.

τίκτω, *bring forth;* τέξομαι, ἔτεκον, τέτοκα.

τιτρώσκω, *wound;* τρώσω, ἔτρωσα, τέτρωμαι, ἐτρώθην.

τρέπω, *turn;* τρέψω, ἔτρεψα, τέτροφα, τέτραμμαι, ἐτρέφθην, ἐτρᾰπην.

τυγχάνω, *hit, happen;* τεύξομαι, ἔτυχον, τετύχηκα.

ὑπισχνοῦμαι, *promise;* ὑποσχήσομαι, ὑπεσχόμην, ὑπέσχημαι.

φαίνω, *show;* φανῶ, ἔφηνα, πέφαγκα, πέφασμαι, ἐφάνθην, ἐφάνην, φανήσομαι; 2nd Perf. πέφηνα, *I have appeared.*

φθείρω, *destroy;* φθερῶ, ἔφθειρα, ἔφθαρκα, ἔφαρμαι, ἐφθᾰρην.

φύω, *produce;* φύσω, ἔφυσα, πέφῡκα, *I am by nature;* ἔφυν, *I was.*

χαίρω, *rejoice;* χαιρήσω, κεχάρηκα, ἐχᾰρην.

χάσκω, *yawn;* χανοῦμαι, κέχηνα, *I yawn.*

χέω, *pour,* F. χέω, A. ἔχεα, κέχῠκα, κέχῠμαι, ἐχῠθην.

χρή (impers.), *there is need.* Subj. χρῇ, Opt. χρείη, Inf. χρῆναι, Imperfect ἐχρῆν, or χρῆν.

χρῶμαι(αο), *use*, χρήσομαι; ἐχρησάμην, κέχρημαι, ἐχρήσθην.

ὠθῶ (έω), *push*, Impf. ἐώθουν; ὤσω, ἔωσα, ἔωσμαι, ἐώσθην.

CHAPTER XVII.

VERBS WHICH FORM THEIR TENSES FROM DIFFERENT ROOTS.

(1) *Speak, say.*

ἀγορεύω, *I say*, and its compounds have Fut. ἐρῶ; Aor. εἶπον; Perf. εἴρηκα; Perf. Pass. εἴρημαι; Aor. ἐρρήθην; Fut. ῥηθήσομαι and εἰρήσομαι.

The Aor. εἶπον is particularly irregular, the Second Person in both Singular and Plural being formed as if from εἶπα. Thus—

εἶπον, εἶπας, εἶπε(ν), εἴπατον, εἰπάτην, εἴπομεν, εἴπατε, εἶπον.

So in the Imperative we have εἰπέ and εἰπόντων, but εἴπατε, εἰπάτω, and εἴπατον. The α does not appear in the Optative, Infinitive, or Participle.

λέγω is more frequent than ἀγορεύω when the simple Verb is required, but ἀγορεύω supplies its place in compounds, λέγω, λέξω, ἔλεξα, ἐλέχθην, λεχθήσομαι, λελέξομαι.

(2) *Take, choose.*

αἱρῶ (έω), *I take*; Impf. ᾕρουν; Fut. αἱρήσω; Perf. ᾕρηκα; Aor. εἷλον. Most of the Passive forms come from a third root.

ἁλίσκομαι, *I am taken*; Impf. ἡλισκόμην; Fut. ἁλώσομαι;

Aor. ἑάλων, ἥλων, or ᾑρέθην; Perf. ἑάλωκα, ἥλωκα or ᾕρημαι.

The Mid. of αἱρῶ has the meaning *I choose.*

αἱροῦμαι, *I choose;* Impf. ᾑρούμην; Fut. αἱρήσομαι; Perf. ᾕρημαι, *I have chosen*, and *I have been chosen;* Aor. ᾑρέθην, *I was chosen;* Fut. αἱρεθήσομαι, *I shall be chosen;* ᾑρήσομαι, *I shall have been chosen;* Aor. εἱλόμην, *I chose.*

Verbals αἱρετός, *that may be taken*, or *that may be chosen;* αἱρετέος, *to be taken*, or *to be chosen.*

(3) *Go, come.*

ἔρχομαι, *I go;* Subj. ἴω; Opt. ἴοιμι or ἰοίην; Imp. ἴθι; Inf. ἰέναι; Partic. ἰών.

Impf. ᾖα, see p. 66.

Fut. εἶμι, see p. 66.

Aor. ἦλθον, ἔλθω, ἔλθοιμι, ἐλθέ, ἐλθεῖν, ἐλθών.

Perf. ἐλήλυθα, or ἥκω, *I am come.*

Plupf. ἐληλύθη (ειν); ἧκον, *I was come.*

The Fut. ἐλεύσομαι is not Attic, but occurs in other dialects and in Tragedy.

(4) *Eat.*

ἐσθίω, *I eat;* Impf. ἤσθιον.

Fut. ἔδομαι; Aor. ἔφαγον.

Perf. ἐδήδοκα; Partic. ἐδηδοκώς or βεβρωκώς.

Perf. Pass. ἐδήδεσμαι, or καταβέβρωμαι.

Aor. κατηδέσθην.

(5) *Live.*

ζῶ, *I live;* see p. 116, § 114.

Subj. ζῶ; Opt. ζῴην; Imp. ζῆ; Inf. ζῆν; Partic. ζῶν.

Impf. ἔζων; Fut. βιώσομαι, rarely ζήσω; Aor. ἐβίων.

Perf. βεβίωκα; Perf. Pass. Impers. βεβίωται.

(6) *Kill.*

κτείνω, ἀποκτείνω, *I kill.*

Fut. κτενῶ, ἀποκτενῶ.

Aor. ἔκτεινα, ἀπέκτεινα.

Perf. ἀπέκτονα.

Plupf. ἀπεκτόνη (ειν).

The uncompounded forms are the rarer, and are quite un-Attic in the Perfect and Pluperfect. Xenophon uses κατακαίνω, κατέκανον and κατακέκονα, but he is not to be imitated. For the Passive Attic writers used the forms of θνήσκω, *I die*, θνήσκω, ἀποθνήσκω; Impf. ἔθνησκον, ἀπέθνησκον; Fut. ἀποθανοῦμαι; Aor. ἀπέθανον; Perf. τέθνηκα, *never* compounded. Plupf. ἐτεθνήκη (ειν), *never* compounded.

(7) *See.*

ὁρῶ (άω), *I see;* Imp. ἑώρων; Fut. ὄψομαι; Aor. εἶδον, ἴδω, ἴδοιμι, ἰδέ, or ἴδε, only in Poet. ἰδεῖν, ἰδών; Perf. ἑόρακα [ἑώρακα], also ὄπωπα; Perf. Pers. ἑώρᾱμαι or ὦμμαι; Aor. ὤφθην; Fut. ὀφθήσομαι.

(8) *Sell.*

πωλῶ (έω), *I sell;* more rarely ἀποδίδομαι; Impf. ἐπώλουν, ἀπεδιδόμην; Fut. πωλήσω, or more frequently ἀποδώσομαι; Aor. ἀπεδόμην; Perf. πέπρακα.

Pass. πωλοῦμαι [πιπράσκομαι rare].

Fut. πωλήσομαι; Aor. ἐπράθην.

Perf. πέπρᾱμαι; Plupf. ἐπεπράμην.

Fut. Exact. πεπράσομαι.

(9) *Consider.*

σκοπῶ, ἐσκόπουν, or σκοποῦμαι, ἐσκοπούμην; Fut. σκέψομαι; Aor. ἐσκεψάμην; Perf. ἔσκεμμαι.

(10) *Strike.*

τύπτω, *I strike, I wound.*

Fut. πατάξω; Aor. ἐπάταξα.

Perf. πέπληγα.

Pass. τύπτομαι; Aor. ἐπλήγην (in compounds ἐπλάγην), Perf. πέπληγμαι; Fut. πληγήσομαι; Fut. Exact. πεπλήξομαι.

But when τύπτω means *I strike with the hand or cane*, different forms are used. Thus: Fut. τυπτήσω; Perf. πέπληγα; Fut. Pass. τυπτήσομαι. The other tenses are generally supplied by a periphrasis, *e.g.*, Aor. Act. πληγὰς ἐνέβαλον; Pass. πληγὰς ἔλαβον; Perf. Pass. πληγὰς εἴληφα.

(11) *Run.*

τρέχω, ἔτρεχον, Fut. θρέξομαι, δραμοῦμαι; Aor. ἔδραμον; Perf. δεδράμηκα, δεδράμημαι.

(12) *Bear, carry.*

φέρω, ἔφερον, Fut. οἴσω; Aor. ἤνεγκα or ἤνεγκον, ἤνεγκ-ας, -ε, -ατον, -άτην, -άμεν, -ατε; Perf. ἐνήνοχα, ἐνήνεγμαι; Aor. ἠνέχθην; Mid. φέρομαι, οἴσομαι, ἠνεγκάμην, ἐνήνεγμαι.

(13) *Buy.*

ὠνοῦμαι, *I buy;* Impf. ἐωνούμην; Fut. ὠνήσομαι; Aor. ἐπριάμην; Subj. πρίωμαι; Opt. πριαίμην; Imp. πρίω, πριάσθω, &c.; Inf. πριάσθαι; Partc. πριάμενος; Perf. ἐώνημαι; Pass. Aor. ἐωνήθην; Perf. ἐώνημαι; Verbals ὠνητός, ὠνητέος.

The Passive Present would be supplied by a periphrasis such as πρᾶσιν εὑρίσκω.

LONDON: R. CLAY, SONS, AND TAYLOR, PRINTERS.

Printed in the United States
125366LV00002B/22/A

9 781436 847384